WITHDRAWN

Twayne's Theatrical Arts Series

Warren French
EDITOR

G. W. Pabst

G. W. Pabst ca. 1962

G. W. Pabst

LEE ATWELL

BOSTON

Twayne Publishers

1977

Published by Twayne Publishers,
A Division of G. K. Hall & Co.
Copyright © 1977 by G. K. Hall & Co.
All Rights Reserved
First Printing

Library of Congress Cataloging in Publication Data

Atwell, Lee
  G. W. Pabst.

  (Twayne's theatrical arts series)
  Bibliography: pp. 155–59.
  Filmography: pp. 161–78.
  Includes index.
  1. Pabst, G. W., 1885–1967   I. Title.
PN1998A3P2622   791.43'0233'0924   77-12898
ISBN 0-8057-9251-1

MANUFACTURED IN THE UNITED STATES OF AMERICA

Contents

About the Author

LEE ATWELL, author of *G. W. Pabst,* was born in Mineral Wells, Texas, in 1941. He studied at Texas Christian University and the University of Southern California, where he received a Bachelor of Arts in Cinema and Liberal Arts, in 1963, and a Master of Arts in Film History and Criticism at UCLA in 1966. He has lectured briefly at San Francisco State University and the London Film School, in England. From 1968 to 1970 he worked as a research cataloger for *The American Film Institute Catalog: Feature Films, 1921–1930,* in Washington D. C. His critical writings on film have appeared frequently in *Film Quarterly* and *Film Journal,* as well as numerous California newspapers and periodicals.

Editor's Foreword

AN INTRODUCTORY STUDY IN English of G. W. Pabst is especially important to this series because as Lee Atwell soundly observes, "Pabst has not been simply underrated as a director as much
as he has not been sufficiently rated at all." For many years Pabst's
reputation has suffered for reasons that are really not related to the
objective judgment of his artistic achievement: his major films were
for years unavailable or circulated only in censored or mutilated
versions; his work in Nazi Germany during World War II made
many enemies and raised many questions about his sympathies, and
much of his work was hasty or trivial.

Yet an artist should be judged by his triumphs not his failures;
and Pabst's undeniable glory is that during the few dying years of
Germany's Weimar Republic from 1925 to 1931, he made at least six
pictures of continuing international importance—*The Joyless Street,
The Love of Jeanne Ney, Pandora's Box, Westfront 1918, The
Threepenny Opera*, and *Comradeship*—a larger achievement than
that on which the reputations of some other celebrated directors,
like Pabst's compatriot F. W. Murnau, have rested. One cannot
suppress the distressing thought that if Pabst had died, like Murnau, during his American visit in the 1930s, he would probably have
a far more glorious reputation today.

Nor can one avoid being distressed by a sense of waste when
contemplating Pabst's career. He spent too much time on mediocre
projects, not because he wished to, but because he had no alterna-
tives. He could not work under pressures like those generated by
the Hollywood "studio system" of the 1930s; but he was not, like his
other great compatriots Fritz Lang and Erich von Stroheim, temperamental or aggressive enough to command his own way. As a
result, Pabst did his best work only on those few occasions when his
genius was respected. (As Lee Atwell points out, even one of the

pictures Pabst made during World War II, *Paracelsus,* and such a late work as *The Last Ten Days of Hitler,* show that Pabst could still produce outstanding work during his later years when he was given a free hand.) Pabst was indeed an *auteur,* in the sense of a creator whose finest realizations are the indisputable products of a unique style and vision. The pity is that Pabst's *authority* was so rarely recognized.

While Lee Atwell makes no pretension of providing a definitive study of a complex artist, he does illuminate the frustrations Pabst often encountered. He offers fresh evidence that begins to explain Pabst's extraordinary situation during World War II, and he separates those projects that really involved Pabst from the hackwork he could sometimes not avoid. Atwell also argues convincingly that Pabst's decline began with his emigration from Germany to even a sympathetic France. Pabst was one of those artists, like novelist John Steinbeck, who derived their strength from a close association with their native soil. Again like Steinbeck, though Pabst's early work often seemed radical, he returned at last to the conservative, patrician, rural traditions of his childhood and a preoccupation with a happier, vanished past.

Atwell is right in comparing Pabst to D. W. Griffith as a moralist; both are essentially nineteenth-century pastoral moralists in their outlook. Nineteenth-century morality has justifiably been viewed with great suspicion in recent years; but if it is responsible for some catastrophic tragedies, it has produced also some transcendent art that still inspires sober contemplation. This book provides a starting point for the appreciation of an artist whose lessons have not so far been sufficiently pondered.

W. F.

Preface

IN OUR CURRENT AGE of director-as-superstar, the cinematic achievement of G. W. Pabst is long overdue for proper recognition. Pabst's name often appears in lists of the cinema's early luminaries, along with men like D. W. Griffith and Sergei Eisenstein, and his early films are cited by film historians who follow precedents in acknowledging their technical skill, psychological acuity, and realism in exploring social themes. Yet, only three brief monographs, in French, have been devoted to him, and students and *cinéphiles* are unlikely to be familiar with many of his films, not to mention the range of a provocative career that spreads from 1923 to 1956.

Pabst's charming and mordant version of *Dreigroschenoper* (*Threepenny Opera*) is popular today principally because of its connection with Brecht and Weill's work; his silent masterpiece *Die Büchse der Pandora* has been revived to capitalize on its radiant young star Louise Brooks; and *Komödianten* and *Paracelsus* have recently become available due to the renewed interest in films produced in Nazi Germany. In addition, much of Pabst's early work is available from the Museum of Modern Art Film Library; yet it may remain difficult for the observer unacquainted with the whole of Pabst's career to understand the artistic or social significance of these films today. Pabst himself, on reseeing some of his early films, felt that contemporary audiences, unaccustomed to the relatively exaggerated idiom of silent techniques, would find them laughable; yet current silent film revivals suggest that after some acclimation, sophisticated viewers are capable of enlightened responses.

Like a brilliant and rebellious child who later fails to fulfill the promise of his youth, Pabst has for some time been viewed as a special, puzzling case, a fallen angel not to be accorded the stature of a Fritz Lang or F. W. Murnau, both his contemporaries.

At the age of 38, following an extensive period of acting and directing theatre in Vienna, Switzerland, and briefly in America, Pabst made his filmic debut with *Der Schatz* (The Treasure), a conservative but accomplished excursion into the realm of cinematic Expressionism. His international reputation was established two years later, in 1925, with *Die Freudlose Gasse* (The Joyless Street), unprecedented in its rendering of the harsh realities of a decadent, inflationary Viennese society. Championed by the intelligentsia and leftist sympathizers, annoyed by censors, and enjoying a certain amount of commercial success, Pabst's succeeding films proved him a significant, controversial artist.

During the late 1920s and early 1930s Pabst became deeply committed to the goals of Marxist social revolution which he introduced into his work. If Pabst had been a novelist, a playwright, or a political journalist rather than a film director, his ideas might have been expressed with more clarity and precision. However, in the framework of an industrial, commercial medium—backed by powerful, conservative finance—social and political views, especially of a revolutionary nature, were necessarily disguised and subdued. The liberated sexuality of *Pandora* or the proletarian sentiments of *Kameradschaft* seem innocent when compared with today's radical film making, yet the most telling clue to their original subversiveness lies in the distortion and mutilation of many of Pabst's films over the years by censors, often totally reversing their meaning and impact. Fortunately, the most important of these have been reconstructed during the past two decades from partial existing prints, and if they sometimes resemble fragments of antique statuary, faded and far removed from the luster of the original, flashes of inventiveness and candor remain for the appreciative eye.

Pabst's immigration to France in 1933, following his successful multi-language version of *L'Atlantide* and the rise to power of Hitler, marks the decline of his career, politically and artistically. After directing an ill-fated but interesting version of Cervantes' *Don Quixote* in France, he accepted an invitation to go to Hollywood, where the stifling conformism forced on him by Warner Brothers produced an unhappy result with *A Modern Hero* and an important, aborted project at Paramount.

When the war that Pabst had so passionately opposed in *Westfront 1918* became imminent, he departed for Switzerland from France. Then, just before the invasion of Poland in 1939, an unfortunate turn of events brought him to the family estate in Austria. Unable to return to America as planned, he was later urged to make films "for entertainment purposes," and while he refused to engage in the propaganda effort supporting the Third Reich, his historical costume dramas, *Komödianten* and *Paracelsus*, were interpreted as evidence of his betrayal by those who earlier admired his staunch resistance to compromise. The lingering suspicion of "collaboration" has continued to prejudice postwar historians who might otherwise have contributed an in-depth study of Pabst.

Added to these problematical issues is the central one of discerning connecting themes and stylistic motifs. Unlike Griffith or Murnau, whose films have a consistency of themes and techniques that support a unified creative world view, Pabst's output is notably diverse in this respect. If certain atmospheric motifs, actors, or techniques recur in some films, Pabst's cinematic ideas are constantly shifting with the circumstances of each production. Although drawn toward social realism in several important films, he was equally fascinated by melodrama which could result in major works like *Der Liebe der Jeanne Ney* or mediocre commercial films like *Gräfin Donelli*, most of which have since been lost and perhaps justly forgotten. While individual films, like *Der Schatz*, may be characterized as Expressionist, Pabst's stylistic fluctuations mingle psychological and impressionistic strains of realism with moments of imaginative quasi-Expressionist stylization. This is true of even the most determinedly realist works, *Westfront 1918* and *Kameradschaft*.

Admittedly, Pabst is not the easiest of filmic personalities to decipher. Many complex, often contradictory, facets of his artistic personality emerge in his career. Unable to resolve the variety of Pabst's work, French historian Henri Agel concludes that "he is the most indefinable of German directors: to the ambiguous and fugitive character of his German temperament is added a strange duality always oscillating from non-realism to objectivity."[1]

The present study, which makes no pretensions to being definitive, particularly as regards Pabst's personal life, offers the student and film enthusiast an introductory appreciation of Pabst's films, his skill in penetrating feminine psychology, his keen appreciation and understanding of editing techniques, and his romantic sensibility underlying his forays into critical "objectivity." It is an invitation to the reader to explore, with all its detours and discontinuities, the unique and fascinating world that Pabst managed to create with film.

LEE ATWELL

Los Angeles, California
October, 1976

Acknowledgments

AMONG THE MANY INDIVIDUALS and institutions helpful to me in the preparation of this volume, I should like to express my sincerest gratitude to Lotte H. Eisner, whose ideas and encouragement opened doors for me; to Herbert Luft, Mrs. Gertrude Pabst, Dr. Agnes Bleier-Brody, Rudolph Joseph, and Marc Sorkin, all of whom provided invaluable information about Pabst's career and life. For arranging for me to see prints of the films, I am indebted to the late Henri Langlois and Mary Meerson of the Cinémathèque Française, the staffs of the Deutsches Institut für Filmkunde and Murnau-Stifftung in Wiesbaden, the Library of Congress in Washington D. C., and individually to David Shepard and William K. Everson. For research materials I would like to thank the libraries of the British Film Institute, London; the Academy of Motion Picture Arts and Sciences and the American Film Institute in Los Angeles.

I am deeply grateful to G. W. Pabst's long-time assistant and friend, Marc Sorkin, for generously examining this manuscript and correcting, from his own personal experience, errors that have crept into published records of Pabst's career over the years.

I am indebted to Elfreide Fischinger and William Moritz who aided me in translating critical passages from German, and special gratitude should be expressed to Arthur Lennig and Warren French, whose enthusiastic attention and numerous suggestions on the manuscript kept my frequently flagging spirit from despair and without whose encouragement this study might never have been printed.

All illustrations in this book are from the archives of the Film Division of the Munich Stadtmuseum, Federal Republic of Germany, and appear with the permission of Enno Patalas, Director of the Photo and Film Museum. I especially wish to thank Annemarie

Vetter of the Film Division for her interest and co-operation in selecting and expediting the delivery of the illustrations used. I wish also to thank Dr. Hans F. Ulherr of the Department of English, University of Munich, for acting as the representative in arrangements to use the Museum's outstanding collection of Pabst materials.

Chronology

1885   Georg Wilhelm Pabst born August 27, Raudnitz, Bohemia.

1902   After having studied engineering, Pabst studies at the Academy of Decorative Arts.

1904–   Begins working as an actor in St. Gallen, Zürich, Salzburg,
1908   and Danzig.

1910   Leaves for New York with Deutsche Volkstheater, directing and acting in German repertory.

1914   Returns to Europe to recruit new actors; interned in a French camp at Brest as an enemy alien.

1919   In Vienna, Pabst assumes directorship of Neuen Wiener Bühne. (The New Vienna Stage)

1920   In Berlin he joins veteran director Carl Froelich and decides to devote himself to the cinema.

1921   Acts in Froelich's *Im Banne der Krolle* with Gustav Diessl.

1922   Assistant to Froelich and scenarist on *Der Taugenichts* and *Luise Millerin.*

1923   Pabst's film directing debut: *Der Schatz* (The Treasure).

1924   *Gräfin Donelli* (Countess Donelli); marries Gertrude Henning.

1925   *Die Freudlose Gasse* (The Joyless Street).

1926   *Geheimnisse Einer Seele* (Secrets of a Soul); *Man Spielt Nicht mit der Liebe* (One Doesn't Play with Love).

1927   *Die Liebe der Jeanne Ney* (The Love of Jeanne Ney).

1928   *Begierde* (Desire) or *Abwege* (Crisis), *Die Büchse der Pandora* (Pandora's Box).

1929   *Die Weisse Holle vom Piz-Palü* (The White Hell of Pitz-Palu), *Das Tagebuch einer Verlorenen* (Diary of a Lost Girl); Artistic supervision of Marc Sorkin's *Moral um Mitternacht.*

1930   *Westfront* 1918, *Skandal um Eva* (Scandalous Eva).

1931 *Die Dreigroschenoper* (The Threepenny Opera), *Kameradschaft* (Comradeship).

1932 *Die Herrin von Atlantis* (L'Atlantide).

1933 *Don Quichotte* (Don Quixote) made in France.
Du Haut en Bas (High and Low) made in France.

1934 Supervision of Marc Sorkin's *Cette nuit-là; A Modern Hero* (U.S.A.); Develped for Paramount *War is Declared,* which was not produced because of government intervention.

1935 Preparation of a film version of Gounod's opera *Faust* in New York (never shot); returns to France.

1936 *Mademoiselle Docteur* or *Salonique, Nid D'Espions* (Mlle. Doctor; Salonica, Spy's Nest).

1938 *Le Drame de Shanghai* (Shanghai Drama); Artistic supervision of Marc Sorkin's *L'Esclave Blanche* (Veiled Brides) with Viviane Romance and John Lodge.

1939 *Jeunes Filles en Détresse* (Girls in Distress). Travels to Switzerland, then to Austria, with plans to emigrate to U.S.A.; stranded in Vienna by injury.

1941 *Komödianten* (Comedians) (Germany).

1943 *Paracelsus* (Germany).
Der Fall Molander (The Case of Molander) (Czechoslovakia), unfinished due to Russian invasion, possibly destroyed.

1947 *Der Prozess* (The Trial) (Austria).

1949 *Geheimnisvolle Tiefen* (Mysterious Shadows). Supervised and scripted Paul May's *Duell mit dem Tod* and supervised A. Hubler-Kahla's *1-2-3 Aus!* for his own production company.

1950 Artistic supervision of Georg C. Klaren's *Ruf Aus dem Ather;* prepared a version of Homer's *Odyssey* for an English-speaking cast (project unrealized).

1952 *La Voce del Silenzio* (The Voice of Silence) (Italy).

1953 *Cose da Pazzi* (Crazy Affairs) (Italy); directed stage productions of Verdi's *Aida* in Verona and *Forza del destino* in Florence.

1954 *Das Bekenntnis der Ina Kahr* (The Confessions of Ina Kahr) (Austria).

1955 *Der Letzte Akt* (The Last Act; American title, *The Last Ten Days*) (Germany); *Es Geschah am 20 Juli* (It Happened on July 20; Jackboot Mutiny) (Germany).

1956   *Rosen fur Bettina* (Roses for Bettina) (Austria), *Durch die Walder, Durch die Auen* (Through the Woods; Through the Fields) (Austria).

1957   Planned projects: the biblical story of Judith, and Lessing's play *Nathan der Weise* (not realized).

1963   Pabst is made honorary president of an International Conference of Schools of Film and Television in Vienna.

1967   Pabst dies on May 29, in Vienna, from an acute liver infection.

1

Pabst's Early Years

GEORG WILHELM PABST was born in Raudnitz, Bohemia (now a part of Czechoslovakia), on August 27, 1885, of Austrian parents, August and Elizabeth. When he was still a child, the Pabsts moved to Vienna where Georg's father was employed with the federal railway system. Following his family's desires, young Pabst studied engineering at a technical school, then opted for a military career; but by the time he had reached the age of twenty Pabst had fallen in love with the theater and against parental protest began studying at the Academy of Decorative Arts. Two years later, in 1906, he began his apprenticeship as an actor on the stages of St. Gallen and Zurich, securing his first major role as Mortimer in Schiller's *Maria Stuart*. Subsequently, he appeared in German repertory in Salzburg, Prague, and Danzig.

Returning to Vienna in 1910, Pabst embarked for the United States with a German language troupe who performed at the Deutsche Volkstheater (now the Irving Place Theatre) in New York, where Pabst appeared in plays of Hauptmann, Schnitzler, and Bernard Shaw. As the theater was controlled by labor unions, the young actor became acquainted with American social problems and met important figures in the Socialist movement such as Upton Sinclair.

Realizing his limitations as an actor, Pabst's interest turned to directing, and early in 1914 he returned to Europe to recruit new actors. Unfortunately, the outbreak of hostilities resulting in war caused him to be arrested as an enemy alien in France and he was detained in a prisoner-of-war camp near Brest for nearly five years. Here Pabst organized a small theater company and produced popular plays in French. He became intimately acquainted with French culture, which he greatly admired throughout his life. Although very little is known about this early period in Pabst's career, it was

19

Albert Steinrück as Balthasar, the bellfounder, in Der Schatz

undoubtedly important in regard to his later film, *Westfront 1918,* and broadened his political awareness.

On his return to Vienna in 1919, Pabst directed a season of Expressionist theatre in Prague, including two controversial plays of Frank Wedekind, *König Nikolo* and *Erdgeist,* the latter to inspire one of his greatest silent films, *Die Büchse der Pandora* (Pandora's Box). The following year he was appointed artistic director of Neuen Wiener Bühne in Vienna, where he was responsible for a number of avant-garde plays such as Sternheim's *1913* and Georg Kaiser's *Hölle weg Erde.* As Pabst's concern with direction sharpened, he became aware of cinema, still a fledgling art at best, and saw in its potential for realism an expansion of current developments in theatre.

In 1920, Carl Froelich, who had been a newsreel cameraman for several years and a pioneer in German film technology, formed his own production company to produce feature films. After acting in a minor role of Froelich's first production, *Im Banne der Kralle,* starring Gustav Diessl, Pabst wrote the screen adaptation of *Der Taugenichts,* from a novel by Joseph von Eichendorff, and also served as assistant director. The same year, 1922, Pabst again worked as scenarist and assistant on an adaptation of Schiller's *Kabale und Liebe,* released under the title *Luise Millerin.* This melodramatic version of Schiller, that had inspired one of Verdi's operas, starred Lil Dagover, Ilka Gruning, and Fritz Kortner, actors who were all to become prominent in film under Pabst's direction.

From his apprenticeship with Froelich, Pabst learned about technical aspects of filmmaking. While Froelich's work was technically good, it remained mediocre and blatantly commercial through his long career. Pabst was aware of this and though he wanted to break away from established convention, all of his silent films reflect to some extent the oversimplification and broad manner that he learned in theater and film. However, Pabst's career was to move in another and far more productive direction than that of Froelich.

Classical Expressionism: *Der Schatz*

For his directorial debut in 1923, Pabst chose a subject in the tradition of the German Gothic by Rudolph Hans Bartsch. It lent itself perfectly to the Expressionist mode of stylization that was given its purest plastic pictorial form in Robert Weine's famous *Das*

Cabinett des Dr. Caligari (1919) and later developed into a more distinctly cinematic form in such major works as Murnau's *Nosferatu* (1922) and Fritz Lang's *Dr. Mabuse* (1922). The relative artistic importance and commercial success of this style of film making encouraged Pabst to pursue its established techniques with which he had become well acquainted in theater. Backing for the production was secured partly from Pabst's mentor Carl Froelich and from his brother-in-law, Dr. Broda, who wanted to help him in launching his career.

Der Schatz (The Treasure) is the only Pabst film that consistently demonstrates the ambience and thematic preoccupations of classical cinematic Expressionism. Set in an imaginary medieval locale, its scale is small with only five characters set against an imposing architecture of bizarrely distorted forms. These reflect the fairy-tale quality of the story created by imaginative designers, Walter Rohrig and Robert Herlth, who had worked extensively in theater and film. Lotte Eisner has provided us with an incomparable evocation of the film's dark and ominous atmosphere:

Pabst used all the Expressionist paraphernalia: the bell-founder's house is squat, round and bulging, with no apparent structure beneath its clayey masses: its ceilings are low and stifling, its main room is like a mysterious crypt. The main influence felt is that of *The Golem:* those thick, rough dilapidated walls, familiar to us already from many a German film, lurk like carnivorous plants ready to devour any mortal who comes close. There are staircases everywhere, and on all sides dark sunken corridors lead off with sudden steps and sharp curves. Here and there in the darkness we perceive a narrow window dimly lighting fragments of a human figure or a gloomy chamber.[1]

The grotesque and asymmetrical contours of this fantastic habitation, situated "on the shadowy edge of an Austrian forest," embody the psychic atmosphere of the melodrama. In the house live Balthasar, a bell-founder; with Beatriz, his lovely young daughter; Anna, his buxom and sentimental spouse; and John, a mysterious and introverted assistant. Gathered around the dinner table, they radiate a simplicity and contentment that bursts into childlike attentiveness when Balthasar recounts the previous invasion of Turks that resulted in the burning of their house, the present structure being constructed on the old foundations. Rumor has it that some

Balthasar the bellfounder and his wife in Der Schatz

soldiers buried a treasure nearby, and though he dismisses this as unlikely, a close view of John's face suggests the idea has taken hold of his imagination with some force.

That same evening, Arno, a young goldsmith, arrives in a nearby village with a design for Balthasar's new bell. In the local tavern, Arno amuses the peasants and their daughters with his guileless charm and tales of adventure that represent freedom from convention and the purity of spirit of a vagabond. The sequence's lightness, conviviality, and natural spontaneity, contrasting with the mysterious, stifling atmosphere of the bell-founder's cottage, demonstrate qualities that later become more prominent in more characteristic Pabst films. Freddy Buache notes that "the *clair-obscur* . . . allows him to put into relief the presence of objects, the weight of things, the material of a table or piece of clothing. These qualities return in several sequences . . . in counterpoint with the fantastic pictorial effects that justify the intrigue."[2]

Arno is enthusiastically greeted by the household the following day and is immediately stricken by the beauty of Beatriz. He encounters a hostile reception only from John, who is jealous of his boyish good looks, intelligence, and artistry. Obsessed by the thought of the treasure, John somnambulistically stalks the labyrinthine corridors of the house by night. When he is secretly observed by Arno and Beatriz, Pabst introduces the first of a series of striking *Stimmungsbilder*, illuminating John's face with a small lamp that penetrates the gloom. Disturbed by his odd behavior, Anna begins frantically searching for new hiding places for money and valuables. As Arno mocks John's eccentric movements at dinner, the embarrassed assistant falls into a stylized, Caligari-like trance, suggesting his emotional state. Armed with a plan of the house, the ingenious Arno, hoping to prove the treasure does not exist, unwittingly reveals its point of concealment in the foundations.

John persuades Balthasar to conspire with him against the boy for a share of the treasure, but their murder plot, filmed against the searing light of the bell furnace, fails due to the intervention of Beatriz. Elated at learning of the discovery of the treasure, Anna joins in the scheming and sends the lovers to the vineyard while she, Balthasar, and John are overcome by greed at the sight of a cache of jewelry and coins. In a contrasting mood, Arno and Beatriz's radiant affection and love are etched with sweet simplicity that avoids awkward romantic convention. While they are in the wineshed making love, John and Balthasar quarrel over the treasure. Their drunken folly abates only with the entrance of the young couple. Shocked by their perfidy, Arno threatens to kill Balthasar, who has already promised John the hand of his daughter for his share of the treasure. He relents, however, at Beatriz's renunciation of her parents; and, as the lovers depart, John struggles with Balthasar over the gold in a moment of Stroheimian intensity. By candlelight in their bedroom Balthasar and Anna gloat over the prospects of their wealth, while John, infuriated at being deprived of his portion, digs blindly into the depths of the cellar, resulting in the collapse of the foundation and a conflagration that consumes all the inhabitants of the house. In the distance, the lovers pass blissfully and innocently over the hill toward a new life.

In terms of Pabst's subsequent development, *Der Schatz* has been unfairly dismissed as "heavy-handed" and atypical of the "true personality" of its director, as if that personality could be easily discerned. Pabst had not yet begun to explore his facility for unusual camera angles, psychological and social realism, or atomized editing. *Der Schatz* is best understood and appreciated as an exercise in style, perfectly adapted to its subject and carefully executed. Its

slow, deliberate rhythms, favored also by Lang and Murnau, and
the lingering on details of the setting and stylized movements of the
actors, the *clair-obscur* lighting, are all elements of a theatrical
Expressionism given plastic form by cinema. The acting styles contrast the sharply full-blown Expressionist stylization of theatrically
trained performers Werner Krauss and Albert Steinrück with the
fresh and spontaneous manner of the lovers, Lucie Mannheim and
Hans Brausewetter. The cumulative Expressionist effect is enhanced
by Otto Tober's brilliant manipulation of light and shadow and
Pabst's dramatic opposition of corruption and innocence, a theme
that he returns to more than once during his career.

Unfortunately, *Der Schatz*, for all its beauty, did not prove a
success commercially. As a consequence, Pabst remained relatively
unknown and found difficulty in continuing to realize his directorial
ambitions. He was approached by actor-director Paul Wegener (*The
Golem*) to develop a period melodrama, *Madame d'Ora*, but
Wegener was ultimately unable to obtain sufficient funding for the
production.

Gräfin Donelli

At the same time, Carl Froelich had been invited by Maxim
Films to direct a vehicle for Henny Porten, whose acting career had
undergone a sharp decline. However, as Froelich was already involved in another production, he recommended Pabst for *Gräfin
Donelli*, a formula melodrama. Desperate for work, Pabst accepted,
making no changes in the given script by Hans Kyser or in the
casting, and shot the film quickly and cheaply. Since no prints are
known to exist today, an account of its artificial and complicated
narrative suggests what difficulties Pabst must have had in maintain-
ing a fine line between *kitsch* and art.

Following the death of a philandering husband, Countess Donelli
(Henny Porten) finds herself in financial difficulty. Ernst Hellwig,
secretary to her uncle, Consul Bergheim, embezzles funds from the
treasury to help her; but, caught in the act by the consul, Hellwig is
forced to sign a confession to be used against him unless he ceases
relations with the countess.

Years later, Hellwig, now executive of a large financial corpora-
tion, is considered for the post of finance minister, but Bergheim, in
charge of forming a new cabinet, rejects Ernst's nomination because
of his past. Meanwhile, Ernst and Countess Donelli have resumed

their affair and are to be engaged, prompting Bergheim to write Ernst, threating him with exposure. His communique arrives just as Ernst is about to depart for a charity ball to announce his engagement. The countess, distressed by Ernst's failure to appear at the ball, goes to his apartment, discovers her uncle's letter, and impulsively shoots her lover. She only wounds him and, upon regaining consciousness, he does not reveal the true facts concerning his past sacrifice for her. Impressed by the nobility of his gesture, Bergheim is won over and refrains from standing in the way of their happiness.

German critics were overly enthusiastic about the performance of Henny Porten, who reportedly reached new, previously untapped intensity under Pabst's direction. Whatever its actual artistic merits, *Gräfin Donelli* proved a financial plum that enlivened Porten's sagging career. The producers were so pleased that they tried to induce Pabst to continue with this kind of film but he declined, not wanting to be categorized as a commercial director. The production's primary significance for him was the association with veteran cameraman Guido Seeber, who was to contribute substantially to four of Pabst's silent films.

His experiences with workers in America, inmates in a prisoner-of-war camp, and social problems in Europe instilled in Pabst a social consciousness and impelled him to material that would engage him in this area. Marc Sorkin, who became involved with him as an assistant and film editor in 1924, had interested him in S. Ansky's play, *The Dybbuk*, about the lost spirit of a Jew that takes possession of a living person. Pabst acquired an option on the film rights but found producers unwilling to back such a subject. Meanwhile, through Sorkin, rights became available to a serialized novel by Hugo Bettauer, a Viennese journalist preoccupied with crime and social exposé, whose writing attracted Pabst. This work similarly met with a cool reception from financiers because of its concern with postwar inflation.

Michael Salkind, a film distributor, and Romain Pinès, both of whom were desirous of becoming film producers, happened to encounter a wealthy businessman in Paris who was anxious to back a film about Jewish life. Recalling that Pabst had an option on *The Dybbuk*, Salkind summoned him to France, where Pabst ultimately convinced them that it would involve too much of a financial risk and persuaded them to invest in the Bettauer novel, *Die Freudlose Gasse*.

The preparations for what was to become Pabst's first major achievement were lengthy and involved. With an initial capital investment of only $40,000, the partners—Pabst, Pinès, Salkind, and Sorkin—engaged scenarist Willi Haas to write a script and signed established performers such as Werner Krauss, Asta Nielsen, and Valeska Gert. Having fallen under the spell of a young Greta Garbo in Mauritz Stiller's *The Saga of Gösta Berling*, Pabst saw her potential for a part in his film and, against the wishes of the other partners, began negotiations with Stiller for her services.

A shrewd businessman as well as a meticulous artist, Stiller drove a hard bargain with Pabst, demanding the then outrageous sum of $4,000 for Garbo, while at the same time forcing him to sign the unknown actor Einar Hanson at the same price and to pay both performers' living expenses. After Pabst had accepted these onerous conditions, Stiller looked at a draft of the script, realized its artistic strength, but advised Pabst that Garbo was too inexperienced to undertake such a complex role. He even offered to release Pabst from the terms of their agreement. Pabst, however, remained unmoved, declaring that he was willing to risk the difficulties involved. The final results, though achieved under precarious and difficult working conditions, proved that his instincts were right.

2

The Silent Period: Toward an Individual Style

The New Objectivity: *Die Freudlose Gasse*

SHORTLY AFTER THE TURN OF THE CENTURY, technological and cultural developments in Western Europe provoked a radical shift in artistic styles and preoccupations. The former emphasis on intense subjective feeling and states of mind was transformed in to a reactionary objectivism characterized by a strongly critical look at the external world. In Germany, the paintings of Max Beckmann, Otto Dix, and Georges Grosz marked a sharp retreat from the inner distortions of Expressionism, emphasizing the individual in relation to the drastic economic and social problems affecting the entire fabric of Germany. In 1924, Gustav Hartlaub, director of the Mannheim Museum, described this new trend as *Die Neue Sachlichkeit*, relating it to a new feeling of "resignation and cynicism after a period of exuberant hopes (which had found an outlet in Expressionism). Cynicism and resignation are the negative side of the *Neue Sachlichkeit;* the positive side expresses itself in the enthusiasm for the immediate reality as a result of the desire to take things entirely objectively on a material basis, without immediately investing them with ideal implications."[1]

Pabst was the first film director to incorporate these new expressive attitudes, reacting against the escapist fantasies that had predominated in German cinema. At the same time, though his initial efforts were praised for their "unstylized reality" (Kracauer), Pabst's sense of social reality was still expressed in terms of melodrama and, seen in retrospect, projects a strong aura of romanticism.

The inspiration for *Die Freudlose Gasse* was a controversial novel by Hugo Bettauer, serialized in Vienna's *Neue Freie Presse*. Its intrigue unravelled against the background of the moral and financial bankruptcy of postwar Vienna, rampant with black-market

Greta Garbo in Die Freudlose Gasse

speculation, prostitution, and the destitution of an aristocracy whose decadence was the recurrent subject of the films of Erich von Stroheim, a director with whom Pabst shared temperamental affinities and with whom he later became acquainted in Hollywood.

For Pabst, a radical change in perspective necessitated a new approach, registered more in new subject matter than in a radical shift of stylistic expression. In France, where the film had its strongest initial impact, one critic recalls: "Before, we had seen Western films, extravagant films, and suddenly, we discovered something overwhelming to me—romanticism appear on the screen, a German romanticism where we found anew Novalis, Arnim . . . then, this reflecting something quite surprising: Germany, after the war, the misery, the decomposition, the morbidity . . . of Germany, but at the same time, extremely alive."[2]

Paul Rotha has suggested that *Die Freudlose Gasse* can be seen on much the same level as Stroheim's *Greed* (1924). Forcing us to look closer at reality, both share much the same cynicism and meticulous concern for truth, acknowledging the seamy side of existence. Yet Pabst never approaches the symbolic Naturalism pursued by Stroheim, seeking rather a concrete, though stylized realism that incorporates along the way tinges of Expressionistic technique and some opulent, melodramatic acting as well as moments of subtlety and restraint.

The historical reality documented in *Freudlose Gasse* is still shaped in terms of melodramatic convention, but for the first time Pabst has situated the intrigue in a social context. As the opening title from Dante's *Inferno* "Abandon hope all ye who enter here," indicates, each level of society is trapped in its own circle of hell. In the winter of 1923, each of the main characters is seen caught up in the disillusionment and chaos of the post-war era. Along Melchior Street, a line of destitute and desperate men and women wait patiently outside the butcher shop for a scrap of meat. Among them are Maria Lechner (Asta Nielsen) daughter of a poor cripple, and Greta Rumfort (Garbo), the daughter of a civil servant, both of whom are turned away with nothing to show for their wait. Beginning with these two characters, Pabst examines the results of the economic crisis on various levels of society, returning to earlier passages for dramatic and visual irony.

In the shabby, meanly furnished flat of her parents, Maria is severely castigated by her crippled father who is forced to depend on his wife's washing to support the house. Cowering before his threats, Maria retreats to the solace of a makeshift bedroom where she daydreams of Egon, a handsome secretary to a wealthy businessman. Greta, on the other hand, lives in a relatively comfortable apartment with her father and younger sister, and resigns herself once again to serving boiled cabbage for dinner, while Madame Greifer (Valeska Gert), a *coutourière* by profession who now survives by unscrupulous means, is welcomed into the butcher's shop.

Contrasted with the misery of the working classes is the milieu of a social élite and wealthy bourgeoisie, thriving on the remnants of a moribund tradition and false security. Its constantly shifting alliances and misalliances, combined with an inherent equation of money and sex as dominant social values, are brilliantly captured by Pabst's *mise-en-scène*.

Immediately recognizable as a villain from his shifty mannerisms, cigars, and curled moustache, Don Alfonso Cañez, an international speculator, is introduced to General Director Rosenow, his ambitious young secretary, Egon Stirner, and Max Lorring's lovely daughter, Regina, along with attorney Lied and his vampish wife, Lia. While Cañez persuades Lorring to join him in a stock swindle, Stirner's attempts to win the love of Regina are terminated by her refusal to accept anyone other than a man of wealth. In a similarly arranged tryst between Stirner and Lia Lied, the latter suggests a quiet, clandestine rendezvous to which he readily consents. The irony culminates in the introduction of Frau Greifer's brothel, functioning behind the respectable façade of her dress shop, with a smoky, licentious atmosphere and claustrophobic décor for which Pabst was to become famous, counterpointed by scenes of the queue in front of the butcher's shop where Greta faints from exhaustion and the butcher flirts with a streetwalker passing his basement window. (At this point, according to Marc Sorkin, a most powerful scene was omitted. Herta Von Walther visits Werner Krauss's butcher shop, and he forces her to make love to him in order to obtain a piece of meat. This episode provides the motivation for her killing him at the end of the film—something missing from the versions currently circulating.)

At Stirner's apartment, Maria learns that his most pressing concerns are financial and agrees to help him acquire funds for an investment. Simultaneously, Herr Rumfort, in return for a monetary concession from his superiors, is induced to resign his position. At the same time, Greta, employed as an office clerk, is taunted by her co-workers. Weakened by her vigilance at the food lines, she is unwittingly victimized by her lecherous employer. Her spirits are temporarily brightened at home by her father's arrival with a miraculous supply of food, though she is unaware that he has invested in the ill-fated stock swindle. At his insistence, Greta goes to purchase a much needed coat at Madame Greifer's. Her haggard countenance is suddenly transformed as she touches and luxuriates in a fur, reaffirming her feminine sensuality. The lighting, photography, and Garbo's natural qualities are combined by Pabst to give us an ineffable moment of cinematic beauty.

Arriving at the same shop, Maria asks for a loan from Madame Greifer and while waiting in a back room is willingly seduced by the wealthy Don Alfonso. A brief scene reveals the meeting between Stirner, the man she loves, and Lia Lied in disguise at a hotel; then after an abrupt shift to Regina and his society friends, news arrives that Lia has been robbed and strangled. Regina recalls the planned rendezvous with Stirner and is convinced of his guilt.

The Rumforts' futures are cast in further jeopardy when Greta is fired for resisting the attentions of her employer and Rumfort is notified of a "crash" in the Petrowitz stock in which he has invested. The ever-indulgent Madame Greifer refuses to buy back Greta's coat but offers to arrange an appointment for her with "a very influential man." A ray of hope appears in the person of Lieutenant Davis, a young American who becomes a boarder in the Rumfort residence and whose money and sincere charm make him a likely prospect for Greta. Hoping to buy off her father's creditors, she keeps the engagement with Greifer and, to her astonishment, the "influential man" turns out to be none other than the local butcher, *nouveau riche* overnight and barely able to suppress his libidinous nature beneath respectable attire and grooming. The subtle humor and incisive detail of this sequence which ends in a stalemate recalls Stroheim's typical juxtapositions of innocence and perversity. Made ill at ease by Greta's modesty and integrity, the *fleischermeister* is contented by a full course meal while Greta after some persuasion agrees to attend Frau Greifer's *soirée*.

Pabst's Expressionist techniques are powerfully brought to the fore in one of the film's most haunting, if atypical, sequences. Maria—now Don Alfonso's mistress—takes him to the hotel where

Two scenes from Die Freudlose Gasse. *Asta Nielsen at top.*

Lia was murdered and confesses her "horrible memory." Asta Nielsen, transformed by a flowing white gown, sparkling jewels, and a shimmering headpiece—all thrown into relief against deep shadow—tells how she witnessed the crime. Her complex succession of stylized movements and dramatic gestures conveys the falseness of her account and strongly suggests her own guilt when she nearly strangles Cañez.

Opposed to these heavy histrionics, the flowering romance between Greta and the young lieutenant is light, fresh, and spontaneous. Then, when Davis finds reason to doubt the family honor, his ardor cools, and Herr Rumfort suffers a stroke. Plagued by poverty, Greta imagines the hand of a workman—a ghostlike superimpression—reaching out for payment. Meanwhile, having deserted Cañez and after wandering through the streets, Maria returns home only to learn Egon is being tried for Lia's murder. Her confession of guilt to the police is succinctly expressed with a flashback to the murder showing only abstract close-ups of Maria's expressive hands.

The troubled situation reaches its climax in the revelry at Madame Greifer's brothel where Greta has reluctantly agreed to make an appearance. As Greta, virtually disrobed before a three-way mirror by an attendant, resigns herself to her fate, slowly brushing her hair before her reflection, we can glimpse Pabst's remarkable talent for eliciting moods and for drawing on the natural depth of an inexperienced young starlet. While escaping the advances of a male customer, Greta finds herself in the main room and is confronted with her purportedly innocent lover, Davis. Each is equally shocked at the other's presence, but recriminations are averted by the arrival of Herr Rumfort, who has traced his daughter there in the belief that she is prostituting herself to save him from debt.

While Madame Greifer introduces an entertainment for her guests, on the street the poor of the neighborhood queue in front of the butcher's shop. Action in both arenas builds to a peak of parallel agitation that climaxes in the murder of the butcher by a young woman denied meat for her child, the death again treated obliquely with simply a brief shot of Werner Krauss' bleeding face rising before a window. As the turmoil reaches its peak, the guests in the brothel scramble for cover. Pabst and his editor Marc Sorkin use a series of swift, sharp images to display chaos and social disruption, even at one point pursuing a character down the street with an hand-held camera. As the tumult subsides, Pabst conveys a desolation and strange melancholy in a series of "still-life" images: a drum and cymbal, smoldering cigarettes and half-emptied beer glasses, shots of the disordered, empty Greifer residence. In the extant version there is an abrupt conclusion with the lovers united before an open window, suggesting a more secure, hopeful future.

Historically, *Die Freudlose Gasse* is important principally for its bleak, unglamorized panoramic vision of an inflationary, corrupt society. Stylistically, its realism has an imaginative rather than a documentary dimension that refines certain features characteristic of German film tradition. Most obvious is its emphasis on the street as a thematic source, a common trait of the *kammerspielfilm* that prompts Kracauer to classify it as one of the "street films." On a more metaphorical note, Barthélemy Amengual notes that "for Expressionism, the *Kammerspiel*, and their posterity, the street is woman, the street is prostitution, the street is destiny. It promises the better and almost always brings the worst."[3] Pabst relieves the street of its more diabolical connotations here, but it remains typically a studio-bound construction rather than the real thing. In this sense, Lotte Eisner is correct in contrasting the exteriors of Griffith's *Isn't Life Wonderful?* as superior in rendering a true image of the period. Griffith's lyrical landscapes and location photography, however, cannot for a moment disguise his Victorian sentiments; and his analysis of poverty conveys none of the social range, psychological ambience, or the anarchic flavor of Pabst's Vienna. Arthur Lennig, in an unpublished manuscript, observes: "Although Griffith went to Germany in 1924 to film 'real life,' he carried with him his sentimentalism. Pabst gets to the heart of the matter while Griffith is calculating effects that belong to melodrama; there is 'The Dying Scene,' the 'Aren't-We-Cute Scene,' and 'The Chase.' All the heartbreak and tragedy of these awful years in Germany were mellowed, sentimentalized and made 'heart warming.' "[4]

Pabst cast his film with contrasting and varied types. Asta Nielsen's grandiose manner, which won her renewed fame, alternates between mannerism and a quieter, more subtle style that Pabst came increasingly to prefer. His use of Garbo, emerging naturally from a more subdued background and lacking the semaphoric methods of theatrical training, is inspired. Her nervousness and lack of experience with any previous director other than Stiller is used by Pabst to advantage, since these qualities fit to perfection the role she enacts. The cameramen, Guido Seeber and Curt Oertel, at first found difficulty in giving Pabst the photographic results he recalled from *Gösta Berling;* but finally the company found that the special emulsion of Kodak Pathé, which they had to secure in Paris, would provide the soft tones needed. Werner Krauss's eyebrow and eye-rolling techniques are still evident in his impersonation of the libidinous butcher as in Robert Garrison's incarnation of Don Alfonso Cañez. Valeska Gert, who was also to contribute to the future work of Pabst, is memorable for her quaint distinctive pantomime as Frau Greifer, and such eminent society figures as Countess Agnes Esterhazy and Tamara Tolstoi are featured prominently with effect.

The impact of *Die Freudlose Gasse* on audiences in 1925 was devastating because of its unsparing depiction of a world foundering in socioeconomic corruption. In its original version, premiered at the Mozartsaal in May 1925, it was ten reels long, but following wholesale mutilation at the hands of censors everywhere, it shrunk to a mere shell of a film. Paul Rotha recalls: "France accepted the film, deleting two thousand feet and every shot of the 'street' itself. Vienna extracted all sequences in which Werner Krauss appeared as the butcher. Russia turned the American lieutenant into a doctor and made the butcher the murderer instead of the girl."[5] The print available today was constructed by the film's original editor, Marc Sorkin, at the request of the Museum of Modern Art Film Library from prints preserved by the Cinémathèque Française and the Cineteca Italiana, following the original shooting script. Sorkin claims that the Italian print even contained new material not filmed by Pabst. Even with much of the integral footage restored, the equivalent of roughly two reels is missing, accounting for a lack of character motivation, particularly in the relationship between Maria Lechner and Egon Stirner, and the abrupt finale.

If it falls short of being ranked a masterpiece, *Die Freudlose Gasse* remains an important landmark in the history of cinema. It firmly established Pabst as a significant director, and it was this film that made Louis B. Mayer sit up and take notice of Garbo, bring her to Hollywood, and transform her into a glamorous icon of legendary fame. At the height of her career when Pabst's name was ironically beginning to fade from memory a post-synchronized version of *Die Freudlose Gasse* with dialogue was released in America (1937), under its original American release title, *The Street of Sorrow.*

Freudian Symbolism: *Geheimnisse einer Seele*

Although Freud's theory and practice of psychoanalysis and his investigation into dreams had exerted a strong influence on the artistic sensibilities of painters de Chirico, Chagall, and Klee, and novelists Proust and Joyce by 1926, his discoveries about the unconscious had little effect on mainstream cinema. German experimentalists such as Fischinger and Hans Richter were preoccupied with abstract form rather than psychology and the major Surrealist experiments of Léger, Dulac, Dali-Bunuel, and Cocteau had not yet emerged from France. Even the most advanced narrative films, such as Abel Gance's *Napoléon* and *La Roue*, remained entrenched in the rudimentary, deterministic psychology of the nineteenth century theater and novel.

Hans Neumann, a prominent German producer of theatrical films at UFA (Universum Film Aktiengesellschaft)—the Berlin equivalent of MGM—had for some time entertained the idea of making a film about Freud through an education subsidiary (UFA Kulture Abteilung). Pabst, who had for years maintained an interest in Freud's work in Vienna had become especially curious about his dream theories. Pabst had already become acquainted with Dr. Nicholas Kaufmann and through him he contacted Neumann and met Dr. Hans Sachs and Karl Abraham, both assistants to Dr. Freud. Thus, with an actual case history as a framework, Pabst, in collaboration with Neumann and Colin Ross, began creating a dramatization that became *Geheimnisse einer Seele* (Secrets of a Soul).

There is a lengthy, opening explanatory title: "In every man's life there are wishes and desires in the unconscious mind. In the dark hours of mental conflict these unknown forces struggle to assert themselves. Mysterious disorders result from these struggles, the explanation of which is the actual work of psycho-analysis. The doctrine of Dr. Sigmund Freud is regarded as important in the treatment. . . ." At a time when Freud's ideas were still fresh and revolutionary, such a prelude, which seems today archaic and simplistic, was necessary for an understanding of the film's basic action. Placed within its proper historic context, this declaration also serves to free Pabst from a clinical, documentary approach and allows the viewer to accept this side of the presentation purely and simply for what it is: the dramatization of a case history.

Following the brief introduction of Dr. Charles Orth, a disciple of Freud, the main action begins in the domicile of Martin Fellman, a chemist, who resides with his wife in a quiet residential area of Vienna. While trimming his wife's hair in their bedroom, Fellman is startled by the scream of a dying woman and accidentally cuts his wife. A crowd gathers in a nearby street and a woman is removed on a stretcher, while a bystander exclaims, "He did it with a razor!" With these brief scenes, Pabst introduces the major themes later elaborated in psychoanalytic terms: the wife's loneliness and her desire for children, Fellman's impotency, reflected in his fear of knives and pointed objects. Seen today by audiences familiar with Dali and Bunuel's *Un Chien Andalou* (1928), the sequence carries much of the same aura of subconscious fear of sharp objects.

At Fellman's laboratory, his impotency is again suggested by his ambivalent affection for a young female visitor and the disturbingly attractive presence of his assistant. Following a brief interrogation regarding the murder in his apartment house, his anxiety increases upon learning of the imminent visit of his cousin Erich, a handsome young explorer, whose gifts of a small saber and a fertility idol symbolize his threatening presence in Fellman's mind. As he retires for the evening, a storm breaks, providing a prelude for his anguished dream.

The oneiric world of the unconscious is exteriorized through every manner of visual and optical distortion: superimposure, camera movement, miniatures, split-screen imagery. The gamut of camera magic and visual poetry discovered by avant-garde *cinéastes* becomes in Pabst's imaginative hands the basis for an Expressionist caesura, but it never lapses into pure exhibitionism. The free, yet related patterns are the cinematic correlatives of the random, yet ambiguous structure of dreams. Although Pabst was not the first to realize the filmic potential of the dream—Griffith, Sjöstrom, and Gance realized the possibilities of this motif and Paul Leni's *Waxworks* and Fritz Lang's *Destiny* give it a fantastic framework, he was among the first to explore the psychological mechanism of the dream, and in exploring the unconscious he gives reign to the irrational and subjective.

Fellman recalls his childhood playmate and cousin Erich in a safari costume, gleefully shooting at him from a treetop; in a futile effort to escape, Fellman darts through space and via a plummeting subjective camera movement, we experience his fall to the terrace.

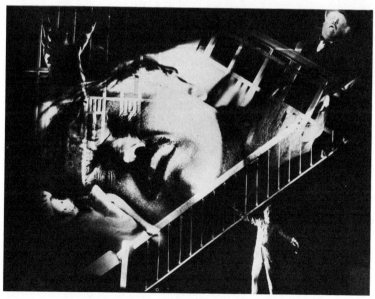

Dream sequences from Geheimnisse einer Seele

Emerging from a cave/womb-like structure in slow motion, he enters the temple of the love goddess Kwanon, passing effortlessly through objects. A complex superimposure of moving trains, snake-like, phallic, and threatening, heralds Erich's impending arrival. Suddenly, Fellman finds himself before a bell tower surrounded by a circular staircase; as he mounts the tower, the bells blend with the "sound" of mocking laughter seen in the faces of his wife, his young assistant, and others. He witnesses a murder, but is rendered powerless to prevent it by a confining iron grid. He is accused of the crime by Erich, and a symbolic trial is represented by the triangular arrangement of Fellman, Erich, and his wife within the frame, preceded by a drummer's shadow and accusing fingers signifying his guilt. From the window of a prison cell, Fellman frantically observes his wife and Erich engaging in a romantic idyll on a moonlit lake. As he begins to attack furiously an apparition of his wife, she awakens him from the dream, but a title informs us that he has forgotten everything.

Preparing for Erich's arrival the next day, Fellman is unable to control his razor while shaving, and at a barber's salon he becomes agitated at the newspaper account of the razor killing. At his laboratory, he cannot force himself to open a letter with a letter opener and drops a test tube upon hearing that his cousin has arrived at home. That evening there is a warm, happy reunion between the cousins and all goes well until Fellman is confronted with the necessity of using a knife at the dinner table. For the first time he shows a marked disturbance and excuses himself.

The slightly ominous atmosphere of the street is brought into play with the meeting of Fellman and Dr. Orth, who are strangely drawn to each other while drinking at separate tables in a cafe. The doctor follows Fellman home, where the chemist discovers he has forgotten his gate key. Orth calms his anxiety with the words: "You have reason for not wanting to enter." And as an explanation of his diagnosis, "I am a psychoanalyst; it is part of my work." Later, Fellman is agitated at the sight of the fertility statue and barely manages to suppress a desire to kill his wife with the saber before he rushes into the street. Seeking refuge with his mother in a moment of childlike regression he confesses the "strange passion" to her and the circumstances of the encounter with Dr. Orth.

Fellman follows her advice and visits Orth in his office, where the doctor gets right to the point: "I can help you, there is a method.

. . ." Wisely, Pabst does not dwell on the method but exteriorizes Fellman's gradual recall of the events that lead to the dream, the dream itself, and the realization of its meaning. In recapitulation of earlier dream fragments, Pabst projects them against neutral backgrounds and reveals new symbolic fantasies. The patient tells of his wife's longing for children; a tree they have planted sprouts forth; a dark room is transformed into a nursery; he dreams of harems and unworthy situations involving Erich, his childhood playmate and his wife. He fills in gaps in his memories, such as recognizing the phallic bell tower as a scene from his honeymoon in Italy, and the vision of water as symbolizing an impending or desired birth. In response to the analyst's classic line, "Did you have a similar experience in childhood?" Fellman experiences total recall, providing the arbitrary but necessary solution to the puzzle—an early experience during a Christmas celebration which left him with an overwhelming sense of rejection. Finally, in the analyst's presence, under hypnosis, he ritually enacts the "murder" he has so frequently contemplated. A didactic title summarizes the salient points of the case, but sentimental convention introduces an unnecessary note in the happy ending, filmed against a bright, country landscape, in which Fellman is reconciled with his cousin and in a moment of delirious joy rushes into the waiting arms of his young child.

For all its premature psychologisms, Pabst's work still maintains the mystery and charm of a poem on Freudian themes. Kracauer's assertion that its subject resembles that of Arthur Robison's *Warning Shadows* is partially justified, but Robison's film, based entirely on Expressionist techniques, owes little to the relative detachment and restraint of *Geheimnisse einer Seele*.

Werner Krauss's usual effusive style of acting is subtly modulated in the framing story, then given full reign in the dream sequences, but Pabst's casting of the psychoanalyst was especially effective. He had seen Pawel Pawlow, a Russian emigré actor, in two films of Robert Weine and was especially impressed with his performance as the Inspector in *Roskolnikoff*. As with Garbo, he instinctively felt Pawlow was perfect for the role. Pawlow spoke only Russian and had no knowledge at all of Freud's work or concepts. Since Pabst's film was silent, language was not an impediment, but Pabst insisted that he become thoroughly prepared and had Marc Sorkin, who spoke fluent Russian, take courses with Dr. Hans Sachs, then translate his notes into Russian for Pawlow during a period of several weeks. He adapted himself to the role so persuasively, in fact, that a group of American therapists later contacted him for a lecture, mistaking him for a bona fide practitioner in the film.

For all the intense acting skill displayed in the film, however, the most remarkable performers are Pabst's cameramen Guido Seeber and Curt Oertel; and the most extraordinary impression is made by the sets designed by Ernö Metzner, whose later short film, *Über-fall*, exploits some of the same optical effects. Six weeks were devoted entirely to work on the dream sequences, which are the heart of the film, made without any of the benefit of the technological advances of the modern optical printer but by the camera itself; they are among the most impressive moments of Pabst's achievement.

UFA promoted the film and released it as a major attraction, and though some bourgeois critics found it obscure and criticized it as detached and without feeling, its association with Freud made it a popular success and it was fortunately not tampered with by censors as much as previous or subsequent Pabst films. In France it was released with the provocative title of *Au seuil de la chambre à coucher* (On the Threshold of the Bedroom).

Man Spielt Nicht mit der Liebe

For some unexplained reason, after the success of *Geheimnisse einer Seele*, Pabst entered into an agreement with Phoebusfilm, a commercial production-distribution-exhibition firm, to direct a film. The relationship did not prove to be a happy one since Pabst—whose inclinations were clearly toward serious, controversial material—and Phoebus could not agree on a mutually acceptable project. Inspired by Eisenstein's masterful *Potemkin*, Pabst wanted to dramatize a historic mutiny aboard German fleet vessels in the harbor of Kiel, but Phoebus wanted to produce another vehicle for Lily Damita, a sultry popular Latin starlet. Pabst suggested Wedekind's play *Die Büchse der Pandora*, but the company considered it too risky. Ultimately Pabst agreed to create an original commercial script for Damita in collaboration with Willi Haas. *Man Spielt Nicht mit der Liebe* dealt with the tearful complications of the daughter of a servant in the court of Emperor Franz Joseph of Austria-Hungary, who falls in love with an elderly gentleman.

Production stills indicate an opulent décor, but no prints appear to have survived, making it impossible to determine the film's visual qualities, though it was photographed by the same cameramen as Pabst's previous two films, Guido Seeber, Curt Oertel, and Robert

Lach. Accounts of the day rated it an indisputable failure due to the inept casting of Werner Krauss—hardly a romantic type—as the old gentleman opposite Lily Damita, who lacked the necessary innocent, virginal qualities.

Revolutionary Melodrama: *Die Liebe der Jeanne Ney*

By 1927 Pabst's tendencies toward the left were sharpened by his involvement with *Dacho,* a German film worker's syndicate, and the following year he joined with Heinrich Mann, Erwin Piscator, and cinematographer Karl Freund, in the *Volksverband für Filmkunst* (Popular Association for Film Art), declaring war on reactionary bourgeois cinema. But he was nevertheless convinced that he could somehow work from within the system and subvert it in spite of differences of opinion. Thus, in 1927, he pursued his ambivalent flirtation with the commercial establishment by persuading UFA to let him film Russian author Ilya Ehrenburg's novel of romance and revolution in the Crimea, *Die Liebe der Jeanne Ney.*

UFA (Universum Film Aktiengesellschaft) which had been under the control of Die Deutsche Bank since its inception in 1917 and which was directed by a group of military men headed by Paul Davidson was at the time undergoing a shift in ownership to the powerful, conservative Hugenberg Press. The board of interim administrators, headed by Ludwig Klitzsch, sought out well-known directors and Pabst accepted their invitation. They must have been unfamiliar with Ehrenburg's novel, since Pabst failed to inform them that it was favorable to Bolshevik revolutionaries. On the other hand, its melodramatic potential included many of the elements of the adventure-spy story mixed with romance so that the studio hoped to capitalize on the current rage over Eisenstein's *Potemkin* as well as the fast-moving, action-packed American film they wished to emulate.

Pabst saw in the material a chance to express his sympathy with Communist ideals and to advance further the critique of European society he had begun earlier. Its action extends from the turmoil of revolutionary Russia to a jaded and sophisticated Parisian milieu, giving Pabst ample opportunity to focus on social conditions. Kracauer sees its value in these terms:

This reality is postwar Europe in full disintegration. Its ghastliness unfolds in scenes which are unique not so much for their unhesitating frankness as for their insight into the symptoms of social morbidity. Such a symptom is, for instance, the mixture of cruelty and obscenity in Khalibiev. Surveying various strata of the population, the film sometimes assumes the character of a report on the diseases of European society.[6]

With the added realism of location photography and the frequent analytical use of psychologically apposite camera angles, Pabst's treatment of the story is highly sensuous and though there were significant changes from Ehrenburg's novel, and some concessions to UFA, it was one of its director's triumphs.

Rather than depend on titles for character exposition, Pabst gives the physical environment, particularly objects surrounding an actor, the role of psychological and spiritual commentary. The film's opening shot perfectly exemplifies this: the camera, panning close up, moves from Fritz Rasp's shabby boots propped up on a table, to a tray of smoldering cigarette butts, up his body to a newspaper covering his face. As a waiter brings his check, the camera dwells on his rather Freudian cigarette holder as he brusquely addresses the waiter. Pabst then explores the Russian cafe milieu with the camera roaming about the convulsive, smoky corners of the room until it discovers the revolutionary hero of the story, Andreas, reflected in a mirror. Without explanation, Khalibiev/Rasp begins delving through a telephone directory while Andreas mysteriously exists by a rear door after changing clothes.

Alternating with scenes of the Bolshevik preparations to take over the city at nightfall, Pabst introduces the heroine, Jeanne, daughter of a French diplomat, who reflects on her unhappy years in Russia as her father writes to his brother of their impending departure. As she absently scrawls the letters PARIS on a dusty window, Andreas catches his first glimpse of her from the street amidst the civil strife. From the same background emerges the unscrupulous opportunist Khalibiev, presenting himself to Ney as a journalist who bargains with him for a list of local Communist agents. Intent upon capturing the attention of the charming Jeanne, Khalibiev deliberately destroys Ney's letter to his brother in Paris which he has been asked to post. A meeting of the revolutionary conspirators in a cafe works out the planned *coup* and Andreas learns of their betrayal through Ney's servant Zacharkiewicz, sympathetic to the revolution. Andreas and his band storm the city and enter Ney's apartment to secure the incriminating list. Visual tension is heightened by chiaroscuro lighting and low camera angles. When Ney refuses to comply he is killed. Jeanne, astonished to learn that Andreas is a Bolshevik,

Edith Jehanne in Die Liebe der Jeanne Ney

rushes forward, while a brief flashback to the lovers' embracing in a woodland indicates their previous involvement.

Following the swift and violent opening action, a brief interlude centers around the headquarters of the victorious Bolsheviks, where Jeanne in a state of shock is given refuge. Against a background of executions and hurried congratulations, Pabst concentrates on Jeanne's disturbed state of mind; her gazing at an aquarium and her reflection in a broken mirror poignantly suggest her sadness and inability to adjust to the loss of her father, her lover's actions, and her own solitude. Though warned against the move by his comrades, Andreas arranges with Zacharkiewicz to have her sent to Paris. Their bittersweet farewell, filmed against the darkened ruin of the city drenched by an early morning rain, is memorable for its impressionistic realism, intensified by a poetic atmosphere.

If the character of Khalibiev represents the corruption of the individual by social conditions, undoubtedly Jeanne's uncle, Raymond Ney, is the epitome of bourgeois decadence, often to the point of caricature. His Paris detective agency is a model of disorder and inefficiency where he indulges in an obscene passion for *escargots* and is pathologically obsessed with money. Irritated by

Jeanne's arrival, he refuses her aid until his blind daughter Gabrielle takes a liking to her, resulting in the prompt dismissal of his aging typist. An interplay of close-ups, without titles, contrasting the avarice of Ney with the moving introduction of Jeanne and Gabrielle, constitutes one of the film's many notable passages.

Simultaneously, Andreas and Khalibiev, now director of a French platinum concession, arrive in Paris. Though Jeanne instinctively distrusts him, Khalibiev entertains a courtship with Gabrielle as an avenue to the Ney fortune. His perfidy is obvious in his cold, mechanical embrace, observed by Jeanne and awakening her suspicion. Meanwhile, Andreas is greeted by Comrade Poitras, a young taxi driver, later sent to find Jeanne and deliver a message from Andreas. The camera's dizzying propulsion, following Andreas's trajectory across a bridge and behind a fence, actively expresses the joy of the lovers' reunion. As Gabrielle gaily announces her engagement to Khalibiev, Pabst cuts away with irony to the would-be fiancé kissing the *eyes* of another girl in a cabaret. The exteriors of Paris streets, the Gare du Nord, and other location photography in Paris reveal a new aspect of Pabst's work, heretofore confined to a studio-constructed décor. Its intoxication with natural light values and atmosphere alone give the film the quality, momentarily, of a little documentary on Paris.

At this point Pabst interweaves the complex strands of the plot. Andreas plans a trip to Toulon to deliver money and literature to a Communist cell (a significant addition to Ehrenburg's story). Jeanne, having repulsed the advances of both Khalibiev and her uncle is banished from the Ney household, but Khalibiev's scheme to marry Gabrielle, kill her, and rob the family vault is disclosed to his cabaret confidante, who later informs on him. At the insistence of the studio, Pabst added a typically American-thriller complication that results in some weak comic gags. Ney becomes ecstatic when approached by an American collector to recover a missing diamond. Subsequently a detective, mistaken for a doctor, discovers the missing gem in the entrails of a parrot!

More to the dramatic point is the depiction of Ney's maniacal greed and paranoia, conveyed through Expressionist acting styles. Following the recovery of the diamond, Ney forgets even Khalibiev, whom he has denounced before his daughter, in arranging to collect the reward. Alone in his office, he caresses the stone, rehearses the exchange with imaginary notes, and, paralyzed with fear, locks his vaults. Again, but more effectively, Pabst employs the thriller technique in disguising the identity of Ney's killer with a subjective camera until the unseen assassin unexpectedly bumps into Gabrielle, who though she cannot see him recognizes the touch of his coat and recoils in horror. In an excruciating and unforgettable moment, Pabst shows her gradual discovery of her father's corpse.

In a contrasting lyrical mood, Andreas joins the abandoned Jeanne and they spend the night together in a small hotel, though, rather charmingly, they do not disrobe and are by implication chaste. From their window, they contentedly spy on a wedding reception where a weeping bride suggests a misunderstanding. Unaware that Khalibiev has implicated Andreas in the robbery and murder of Ney, the momentarily enchanted lovers wander through an open marketplace; and during a brief visit to a church, Jeanne implores Andreas not to undertake the mission to Toulon. But he is arrested before Jeanne can summon Khalibiev as his "witness" to his whereabouts and she frantically follows the villain to the Gare de Lyons. Trapped inside a railway car, Khalibiev agrees to her terms, but attempts to force himself on her sexually. In the ensuing struggle the train stops and she discovers the incriminating diamond. With the arrival of authorities, Khalibiev is exposed by Jeanne and pursued into the countryside, while Jeanne's face, reflected in a close-up of the jewel, blends into the final liberation of her lover Andreas. With this Expressionist touch, Pabst once again expresses—in one stunning romantic image—the mythic triumph of love over corruption and wealth.

Although Ehrenburg was distressed over the dilution and transformation of the political message of his book, UFA officials under the new Hugenberg regime found Pabst's version too radical and initially thought of not releasing it. Rather than lose their considerable investment, however, they finally did so to enthusiastic audience response and critical acclaim.

Much attention has been paid by film historians to the editing style developed by Pabst and his editor Marc Sorkin in *Jeanne Ney*. The transition from one shot to another is frequently effected on a pronounced movement, thus leading the eye naturally from one point to another. Taking an opposing aesthetic position to that of Eisenstein, whose dialectical opposition of shots created a metaphorical concept, or Pudovkin's associational montage, Pabst aimed at creating a rapid and continuous flow of visual movement that owed

little to German film tradition, though Walther Ruttmann's poetic
evocations in *Berlin* must also have been an influence. Pabst's analytical breakdown of a scene seems, in retrospect, simply to give the
film an artificial sense of movement and excitement "in the American style," that helps to obscure the machinations of its melodramatic action. Equally impressive are the fluid, skillful moving camera
shots of Fritz Arno Wagner, following players and roving freely
through sets and locations.

The acting styles in *Jeanne Ney* again display a varied repertory of
mannerism and realism. Like the young lovers in *Der Schatz*, Edith
Jehanne and Ugo Henning are fresh and natural in their dramatic
inflections, contrasting with the overstated, if equally memorable
performances of Fritz Rasp as the villainous Khalibiev, Adolf Edgar
Licho as Raymond Ney, and Siegfried Arno as a detective. Brigitte
Helm, who was to star in Pabst's next film, gives one of the best
performances of her career as the blind Gabrielle, brilliantly con-
veying a complex pathos, and Vladimir Sokoloff etches the first of a
series of exquisite cameos as a revolutionary pal of Andreas.

Jeanne Ney will seem to some viewers nothing more than an
edifying museum piece, but throughout its twists and turns Pabst
interpolates his close-range study of the moral and spiritual climate
of his day. The degree of psychological realism seen in the heroine
and the intensity of its images linger after one has forgotten
the plot.

Abwege

In 1928, a small company, Erda Films, combined the talents of
Pabst with Brigitte Helm for *Abwege* (Crisis), also sometimes known
as *Begierde* (Desire). Though it is not a major work, it demonstrates
Pabst's preoccupation with feminine psychology; but it is rarely
seen today, being available only through European film archives.

The basic intrigue involves a woman, neglected by her successful
husband, who decides to step out with more exciting types, but in
the process discovers after a nearly disastrous divorce that she does
in fact love her husband. Applying his acute knowledge of camera
angles and rhythmic editing, Pabst turns this woman's magazine
fantasy into an interesting meditation on the phenomenon of
bourgeois marriage.

Hans, a reputable young lawyer, marries Irene and fits her into
the accouterments of bourgeois luxury, even taking on more work to

sustain their position. Irene, however, becomes infinitely bored with the solitude imposed on her and seeks companionship with Liane, an inventive and promiscuous girl. One day Liane introduces her to Walther, a painter who secretly begins a portrait of Irene; their friendship develops into love and Irene plans to leave her husband. Hans, however, learns of the relationship and convinces Walther not to meet her at a railroad station. Although he succeeds in establishing contact once again with his wife, she is angered and hurt when he is called away on business. At a Latin nightclub with Liane and her friends, Irene is reunited with Walther, but under the influence of alcohol she is repulsed by Walther's vulgarity and accepts the advances of a boxer. Unable to survive a second crisis, Irene and Hans divorce, but following the separation, Irene realizes her affairs are a delusive flight from reality and Hans ultimately assumes his neglected role of lover and provider.

As in *Jeanne Ney*, Pabst concentrates on environment, but there is no marked fluctuation into Expressionist visual techniques. Most of *Abwege*'s visual interest derives from a fluid moving camera giving its settings and performers a graceful, elegant impression. But, as Paul Rotha writes, *Abwege* is chiefly memorable for Pabst's use of Brigitte Helm: "Her vibrant beauty, her mesh of gold hair, her slender, supple figure were caught and photographed from every angle. The intensity of her changing moods, her repression and resentment, her bitterness and cynicism, her final passionate breakdown in the Argentine club; these were constructed into a filmic representation of overwhelming power . . . Her curious, fascinating power has never been exploited with such skill. Gustav Diessl, as the husband, was beyond reproach, his whole outlook being enhanced by low-level camera angles."[6]

Bringing imaginative skill and sensitive treatment to ordinary material, Pabst proved himself capable of directing a work of quality, and his absorption with his leading actress (who appears later in *L'Atlantide*) leads to Pabst's fruitful association with Louise Brooks.

3

The Years with Louise Brooks

The Liberation of Love: *Die Büchse der Pandora*

IN GREEK MYTHOLOGY, Pandora is the first mortal woman, sent to earth by the gods as punishment for Prometheus' insolent theft of fire. Wisely, the gods endow her with the most alluring yet treacherous of gifts: Athena instructs her in female skills, Aphrodite gives her beauty and fascination, and Hermes inspires her with a desire to please. But she also brings with her a box containing all human ills; when she finally succumbs to temptation and opens it, they all escape, excepting hope—and thus the gods have their revenge on man.

At the turn of the century, Pandora was immortalized as Lulu, the eternal temptress, by the Swiss German dramatist Frank Wedekind, in the plays *Erdgeist* (1895) and *Die Büchse der Pandora* (1905). Aside from Wedekind's mastery of Expressionist theatrical techniques, his graphic use of sexual themes and psychology, and his portrayal of Lulu as an alluring, all-consuming monster who is only checked by the most famous of sexual psychopaths, Jack the Ripper, provoked outcries of moral indignation and scandal from every quarter and the plays frequently were banned from European stages.

Having directed *Erdgeist* (Earth Spirit) on the stage, Pabst had always contemplated making a film centering on Wedekind's fascinating psychological portrait. It had already been made along theatrical Expressionist lines by Leopold Jessner in 1923, with Asta Neilsen as Lulu. The depiction of Lulu's sexual passion was subsumed into broad conventional, socially acceptable, theatrical mannerisms that dampened its subversive, erotic dimension. Interested in a more realistic approach, Pabst wanted an actress whose natural temperament and physical appearance would correspond to his vision of Lulu.

Marc Sorkin, Pabst's assistant and long-time associate, recalls saying to Pabst, "if you find the perfect actor for the rôle, you have the film."[1] Never was this truer than in the instance of Lulu. Pabst had already considered using the young Marlene Dietrich but soon realized that she totally lacked the quality of freshness and innocence he was seeking. Her sultry demimondaine character would merely sensationalize an already provocative rôle. Then, in early 1928, as production plans began to take shape, Pabst saw a young American actress named Louise Brooks, in Howard Hawks' *A Girl in Every Port* and William Wellman's *Beggars of Life*.

Hailing from Kansas, Louise Brooks was a veteran dancer of George White's *Scandals* and the *Ziegfeld Follies*, who possessed a natural grace, a piquant smile, and cropped coiffure that became the inspiration for the comic strip character Dixie Dugan. Between 1925 and 1928 she worked as a contract player for Paramount in a series of films that did not fail to draw applause for her bewitching presence. In spite of her popularity, she was never considered a "serious" actress, capable of playing anything other than a dancer or a flapper though she had occasion to prove otherwise.

Pabst, however, was able to perceive in her an actress whose sense of movement and gesture, instinctive, yet intelligent, fused with a naturally erotic, yet tantalizingly innocent allure that was precisely right for the fatal attractiveness of his Lulu. Meanwhile, in Hollywood, having just completed *The Canary Murder Case* in 1928, Miss Brooks found herself being used as a pawn in the shuffle between silent and sound production at Paramount. B. P. Schulberg refused her the salary increase called for in her contract because the studio had doubts about her "talking" ability. Rather than accept this indignity, Miss Brooks immediately accepted Pabst's offer to come to Berlin. Recalling her astuteness, she offers considerable insight into this fateful and miraculous conjunction of actress and director:

In Hollywood, I was a pretty flibbertigibbet whose charm for the executive department decreased with every increase in my fan mail. In Berlin, I stepped to the station platform to meet Mr. Pabst and became an actress. And his attitude was the pattern for all. Nobody offered me humorous or instructive comments on my acting. Everywhere I was treated with a kind of decency and respect unknown to me in Hollywood. It was just as if Mr. Pabst had sat in on my whole life and career and knew exactly where I needed assurance and protection.[2]

Reflecting on her youthful experience with the great director, she offers much insight into Pabst's methods of dealing with actors and his special understanding of her own abilities. "Unlike most directors, Mr. Pabst had no catalogue of characters with their emotional responses. D. W. Griffith required giggling fits from all sexually excited virgins. If Mr. Pabst ever shot a scene showing a virgin giggling, it would be because someone was tickling her. It was the stimulus that concerned him. If he got that right, the actor's emotional reaction would be like life itself—often strange and unsatisfactory to any audience used to settled acting conventions."[3] She notes that critics of the day complained because she did not go through the contortions of suffering exhibited by Sarah Bernhardt in *Camille*. Pabst apparently contrived to put her in everyday situations from time to time to see how he could elicit the response he wanted. "With an intelligent actor," recalls Miss Brooks, "he would sit in exhaustive explanation; with an old ham he would speak the language of the theatre. But in my case, by some magic he would saturate me with one clear emotion and turn me loose. And it was the same with the plot. Mr. Pabst never strained my mind with anything not relating to the immediate action."[4] The exquisite liberation of Louise Brooks under the patient and understanding guidance of G. W. Pabst is one of the more fascinating areas of cinematic iconography, as French historians Lotte Eisner and Ado Kyrou have demonstrated, and the initial fruit of their relationship is one of Pabst's masterpieces, *Der Büchse der Pandora*.

Like Strindberg, whom he met in Paris, Wedekind was obsessed with the destructive power of sex and sexual anomalies as manifest in terms of female psychology. His original idea for the character of Lulu emerged from a Grand Guignol pantomime; and reacting against German Naturalism, his style was full of flamboyant theatrical devices and his dialogue passion-ridden with phrases that attempted to give artistic form to depth psychology. Wedekind never intended Lulu to be a real personage but a "personification of primitive sexuality" who unknowingly drives man to evil. Wedekind's conception of "evil," was naturally derived from a bourgeois morality that viewed sex as a dangerous, sinful, and unhealthy practice outside of marriage and procreation but which nevertheless yielded an enormous and frequently morbid fascination. Thus the feelings that Wedekind's Lulu evoked were very real and cast a lingering spell upon the Central European imagination for some time.

In 1928, the same year that Pabst began work on his film, Alban Berg, the Viennese protégé of Arnold Schoenberg, who had developed a mature and personal language via atonality and serial technique, began composing an opera to be called *Lulu* on precisely the same sources as Pabst. While incomplete at the time of Berg's death, the opera has been acknowledged as a twentieth century masterpiece and though his libretto is simply an abridged version of the Wedekind plays, it is the searing intensity of the music expressing the drama's emotional peaks that makes it an unforgettable experience. Whereas Berg, in an operatic context, properly heightens the exaggerated theatricality of these plays, Pabst's scenarist Ladislaus Vajda reshaped their violent action, moralistic dialogue, and Expressionist peripeteia, to a more naturalistic treatment that eschewed hypertheatrics for more subtle and intimate cinematic effects.

Wedekind's "tragedy of monsters," *Die Büchse der Pandora,* has a prologue in which a circus animal trainer—who serves as a narrator-chorus—introduces the audience to various animal performers, among them Lulu. This sensational, yet theatrically effective framing device is used by Berg to open his opera, but nothing of the sort is even hinted at in Pabst's film. The action of *Erdgeist,* which deals with Lulu's early career as a flower girl, her marriage, and various lovers of both sexes has been largely reduced to her relationship with Dr. Schön, only briefly introducing her affairs with Schigolch, Rodrigo, and Alva Schön, and eliminating her husband and the artist who paints her portrait. Pabst's surviving shooting script indicates that scenes were originally planned to detail Lulu's earlier life but subsequently deleted.

An early critic in *Close Up* outlined the essential parts of the filmic structure as follows:

I.   Exposition: Lulu and her friends.

II.   Contra Exposition: Dr. Schön's world and the house.

III.   Development of the Conflict: Lulu's debut on the stage and Dr. Schön's defeat.

Following the screen credits, the action begins in *medias res* with Lulu installed in a fashionable apartment entertaining her former protector and lover Schigolch, a crochety but amiable sugar-daddy still dazzled by her charm and beauty. Pabst frequently uses his cutting-on-movement technique to emphasize her flowing gestures as she flirts with a gas man who arrives to check the meter, kneels before the elderly Schigolch, then breaks into a capricious, frenzied dance before her painted portrait in the background.

Schigolch scolds Lulu for deserting him for Schön, a newspaper tycoon, but like all her "friends," he remains a devoted slave. From the balcony he points out her future associate, Rodrigo, a muscular athlete. Lulu is forced to conceal Schigolch when Dr. Schön unexpectedly arrives to announce his plans to marry the daughter of a city official. Lulu jealously forces him to submit to her advances, but when he discovers the presence of the noisy, drunken old man Schön departs in a fury. Passing him in the hallway is the boisterous Rodrigo who meets Lulu, flexes his muscles, and provokes an admiring laugh from her as she swings on his arm like a playful child unrepressed in its affections.

In a brief sequence, Pabst shows us the pretty, conventional daughter of a minister preparing wedding announcements. She refuses to hear her father's objections to the slander circulating about Schön's affair with Lulu. Subsequently, in the Schön residence we meet the handsome young son, Alva, composing his new musical revue at the piano. The Countess Geschwitz enters the room with a portfolio of costume designs. She inquires about Lulu and as Alva is about to explain the predicament, they are both delighted to see Lulu bounce into the room to inform them enthuiastically that Rodrigo Quast wants to do a variety act with her. Lulu's spontaneous embrace of Alva confirms the elder Schön's jealousy and his possessive desire for her seductive charm. "Alva," says Lulu, "is my best

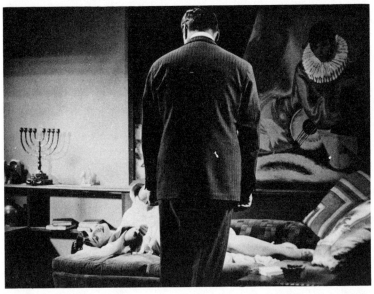

Louise Brooks as Lulu in two scenes from Die Büchse der Pandora

friend—he's the only one who never wants anything from me. . . ."
Countess Geschwitz's silent, stony expressions throughout show her
mixture of embarrassment and jealousy at the display of affection.

When Lulu encounters Dr. Schön in the study, she pretends to
have come to see Alva, kisses him in front of his father, and invents a
prearranged rendezvous. After her flighty departure, Alva suggests
to his father that he might marry her, but Schön barks back, "One
does not marry women like that!" Learning of her plans with Rodrigo, he schemes a diversion by persuading Alva to include her in
his new musical revue; but he concludes with a note of menace,
warning Alva not to become involved with Lulu.

Both Lotte Eisner and Louise Brooks have remarked on Pabst's
brilliance in recreating the milieu of backstage life with its constant
agitation and movement. Here he seems closer to the impressionist
atmospheres of Max Ophüls or Jean Renoir than to his German
contemporaries. Amidst a flurry of provocative and scintillating costumes and elaborate scenery, Peter Schön introduces his fiancée to
the backstage personnel and to Lulu as she emerges from shadow in
a low-cut, shimmering black costume. Sulky and impetuous, she
becomes thoroughly indignant at being subjected to this humiliation
and refuses to go onstage, venting her wrath on the makeup man by
backhanding a powderbox in his face. In the dressing room Schön
reprimands her; and in the ensuing struggle Lulu's hypnotic beauty
conquers the man's physical strength, as she subdues him in an
embrace. Here a standard romantic cliché is transformed into a
poetic visual phrase by Pabst. With a triumphant laugh, Lulu makes
her stage entrance, while Schön broods over a flower. . . .

Lulu's supreme victory lies in marrying into respectable society
and money, as she does when she finally captures Schön. Yet, she
remains the image of innocence at her wedding reception where she
dances with the Countess Geschwitz, whose lesbian sensibility is
made clear (In her essay, "Pabst and Lulu," Louise Brooks amus-
ingly recalls that Pabst had to coax the scene from Alice Roberts,
who was repulsed at having to make love to a woman.) As Lulu joins
Schigolch and Rodrigo, there is an abrupt shift to a darker, quasi-
Expressionist style, as the trio strew roses on the bed in the bridal
chamber and revel in a drunken orgy with deep shadows surrounding them. Alva discovers them and threatens Rodrigo, but is restrained by Lulu, to whom Alva finally declares his love, while his
father remains in the reception hall.

Just as his previous fiancée has discovered him with Lulu in the dressing room, so Schön finds his son in a compromising situation with Lulu, his head suggestively slumbering in her lap, her virginal white gown captured in glistening highlight. As she begins to disrobe, Schön denounces her as a perverse creature whose beauty must be destroyed, gives her the revolver with which he has chased her friends away, and commands her to put an end to her life.

Pabst's use of mirrors and the fragmentation of the scene through editing that suggests more than it shows are well described by Lotte Eisner. "Lulu, wearing the wedding-dress, looks at herself in the mirror and then leans forward to put down her pearl necklace; while she does so, and her image leaves the mirror, the threatening figure of Dr. Schön is framed in the glass. Lulu straightens up, and her image meets that of Dr. Schön who has decided to kill her. Pabst then cuts very briefly to a struggle for the revolver; Lulu is seen from behind, we perceive a puff of smoke and realize that the gun has gone off. Then we have all the details of Schön's death throes, shown from dramatic angles."[6] The scene ends on a symbolic note as the camera pans to encompass a large and prominent sculptural relief of an angel in supplication which has been hovering over the background of the family tragedy, expressing Lulu's ironic mixture of guilt and innocence as Schön's body collapses in a heap between the stunned Alva and Lulu.

Contrasting with her white wedding attire in the preceding sequence, Lulu appears at the court hearing draped in black silk, but when she tries to win over the judge with a radiant smile, our impression is hardly that of a grieving widow. In his testimony the prosecutor draws the parallel between Lulu and the mythical character of Pandora showering evil upon mankind. The smile on the defense counsel's face indicates how insubstantial he finds the argument. The request of the death penalty summons up a seething turbulence in the court room, especially among Lulu's friends— commandeered by Geschwitz, who speaks out vigorously on her behalf. She is turned out, however, amidst cheers and jeers from the animated crowd. While the judge is reading the verdict and the sentence of five years' servitude for manslaughter, Geschwitz and Lulu's cohorts engineer a general panic by setting off a fire alarm, allowing for Lulu's escape. (In Wedekind's play, Lulu is imprisoned but escapes via a complicated ruse involving change of identity and clothing carried out as a sacrificial act by the countess.) Visually, we are left with the impression of a violent storm passing over the room, leaving destruction in its wake.

Lulu returns to the Schön residence, which has been readied for a period of absence. Here Pabst creates some seemingly insignificant but psychologically relevant bits of business that Louise Brooks brings to perfection. At a small table she calms her nerves with a much-needed cigarette; she removes the widow's bonnet after gazing in a mirror; she aimlessly picks up Alva's passport, then begins leafing through a fashion magazine. She finds happiness and consolation in photos of women bathing at the seaside. She runs through the house to the bedroom where the marriage bed and the baroque sculptural pattern momentarily recall the recent tragedy, but Lulu turns her thoughts to the present, luxuriating in the feel of a fur coat, then the rush of tap water in the bathroom.

Alva bursts into the bedroom, bewildered and astonished at Lulu's presence in the house, clutching at her widow's bonnet. Lulu petulantly takes the hat from him and flings it across the room where it falls against the sculptured figure, a grim reminder of Schön's death. Her seductive body, still wet from the bath, and her coy primping before the mirror fail to seduce the guilt-stricken youth; but when Lulu phones the prosecutor and threatens to give herself up, a violent struggle from Alva prevents her from doing so and his resistance gives way to a burning, desperate, passionate embrace, while Lulu whispers, "Let's run away together. The Countess will lend me her passport. . . ." Aboard a train for Paris, they encounter Casti-Piani, a suave pimp, who recognizes Lulu from a news photo, and is induced to join them as the price for his silence. He convinces them not to go to Paris but rather to join him at a place where "the people are hospitable . . . and know how to keep their mouths shut."

Lulu and Alva's subsequent adventures are all condensed by Vajda into events in a single, typically Pabstian setting: a ship converted into a waterfront gambling den whose smoky contours and cosmopolitan ambience prefigure a similar setting later created by the same set designer, Andreiev, for *Dreigroschenoper*. Reunited with her parasitic entourage of Schigolch, Rodrigo, and especially Countess Geschwitz, through whose eyes we are introduced to the milieu, Lulu is urging Alva to try his luck at the gaming tables, but he consistently loses. Using her charm to play one off against the other, she induces Schigolch to aid Alva with a trick card and coaxes the countess into a loan; then, threatened by Rodrigo, who still lays claim to her, she persuades Geschwitz to make advances to him. The shadowy intrigue reaches a violent climax with Alva exposed at cheating, Rodrigo discovered murdered by Geschwitz, and Lulu's rejection of Casti-Piani's attempt to sell her to an Egyptian cafe owner as a dancer. With the arrival of the police, Lulu and Alva manage to extricate themselves from the nightmare and, with the help of Schigolch, escape in a rowboat.

The final act of Wedekind's play is drastically reduced by Pabst and Vajda to only four characters. In London, at Christmas time, Lulu and Alva are living in an attic in desperate straits. Only a brief visit from Schigolch, bearing some seasonal spirits, breaks the atmosphere of gloom. The Expressionist milieu, typical of many German films of the period, is brought into dramatic focus as a mysterious figure in hat and overcoat stalks the lonely, fog-drenched streets of London. The secure warmth of a family glimpsed through a window happily celebrating causes him to be more aware of his cold, solitary condition. He lingers at a Salvation Army station, where tea is being distributed and contributes some money to a pretty young recruit. She offers her assistance, noticing his bleak, lonely countenance, but he refuses with the words: "Nobody can help me! I cannot be helped!" With a smile, she offers him a sprig of mistletoe which he accepts, then wanders again into the fog. With this simple, warm exchange Pabst dispels the tone of melodramatic menace and establishes a symbolic motif with the Salvation Army, all new inventions of the director and his scenarist. Reduced to prostitution, Lulu descends into the night to save herself from starvation/loneliness/desire, followed by the remorseful Alva. Appearing as a shadowy silhouette from a blanket of mist, the stranger (Jack the Ripper) is accosted by Lulu on a streetcorner, but hesitates to follow her up the staircase to their rendezvous. Here, in a classic Expressionist peripeteia, Pabst lingers on disturbing psychological detail, stretching it to subjective proportions. In close-up, Jack's face slowly changes from a semblance of rapture to fear as Lulu's entreaties become more persuasive. Pabst cuts to a close-up of his concealed knife, glistening in the darkness; finally, as Lulu's trust and innocence calm him, he drops the weapon, relinquishing for the moment his desire to kill.

In the attic room, their faces bathed in warm light, Lulu and Jack, two equally destructive and spiritually lost souls, radiate a deceptive tenderness in their embrace; and with a gesture of sincere beneficence, Jack gives her the branch of mistletoe. A bread knife on the table, lit and composed with the care of a still-life, shows how Pabst can invest objects with psychological reverberations as Jack stares at it. In a series of close low-angle shots, he reveals the smoldering glimmer in Jack's eyes, while Lulu, in reverse angle, is seen luxuriating in the ecstasy of the fatal embrace. The murder itself is suggested, like all violent action in the film, by indirect abstraction: close-ups of the glistening knife falling, followed by Lulu's hand falling limply from Jack's shoulder. Pabst concludes with an epilogue of the Salvation Army band marching through the streets, singing carols; and, as Jack passes into the night, Alva Schön is seen quietly sobbing among the crowd, sustaining the tragic tone of the dramatic finale.

Critics of the day were not too enthusiastic about Pabst's *Pandora*, not only because he seemed to be retreating from the sociopolitical themes of *Die Freudlose Gasse* and *Jeanne Ney*, but because they believed that Wedekind's Lulu could not be adequately conveyed by silent screen techniques. As A. Kraszna-Krausz bluntly phrased it, "Lulu is inconceivable without the words that Wedekind makes her speak. These eternally passion-laden, eruptive, indiscriminating, hard, sentimental and unaffected words stand out clearly against her figure. . . . The film is unable to reproduce the discrepancy between Lulu's outward appearance and her utterance. . . ."[7] What these critics could not concede was that the literary, theatrical conception of Lulu was necessarily simplified and transformed in accord with the requirements of a fundamentally *visual* medium. Whereas Wedekind intended "to depict a woman's body by the words she speaks," Pabst uses the body of Louise Brooks as the focal point of expression, employing his talent for revealing psychic states and relationships through camera angles and editing. Whereas Wedekind's spectacle reveled in Expressionist stylization, using character and words as symbols to represent his Lulu as a devastating female monster, Pabst's film reincarnates Lulu as a modern myth. Pabst sees her as a dangerously free and alluring innocent, without any notion of sin in the Christian sense, and only vaguely aware of the moral consequences of her behavior. The tragic contradiction in the film emerges from the discrepancy between her natural unbridled eroticism and its consequences on the behavior of those who fall under her spell.

As indicated by the previous notation of the film's seven essential
parts, each section is developed like a movement in a musical pattern, with its individual tempo, key, and atmosphere. Beginning
with a straightforward, uninflected style, Pabst gradually evolves an
increasingly darker Expressionist texture in Schön's murder and his
treatment of the backstage milieu, culminating in the flamboyant
trial scene and the fast-moving gambling den sequence; then, with
the introduction of Jack the Ripper in London, the visual dynamics
are dictated almost totally by Expressionist themes and lighting
patterns.

In addition to the incomparable performance that Pabst elicited
from Louise Brooks in the central role, *Pandora's Box* owes much of
its finesse to a gallery of exceptional supporting players. There is
again an alternation between an arched semaphoric manner and a
restrained naturalism. Fritz Körtner's Dr. Schön and Kraft-
Raschig's Rodrigo clearly derive from the schooling of melodrama,
while Franz (later Francis) Lederer's sensitive rendering of Alva
Schön, Karl Goetz's happy-go-lucky Schigolch, and Alice Roberts as
the lesbian countess, still strike us as vibrant, naturalistically conceived characters as a whole, contrasting with their sentimental and
often grotesque literary counterparts.

Though *Pandora's Box* is conservative in the context of our contemporary permissiveness regarding sexual themes, it was considered too explicit for 1928 audiences and was cut, distorted, or
banned when initially released. Schigolch became Lulu's adopted
father; Alva, an orphan with no relation to Dr. Schön; Geschwitz's
lesbianism was eliminated so that she became only a "devoted
friend." Pabst's Lulu struck too close to the prevalent vein of sexual
hypocrisy in the lives of European bourgeoisie whose hoard of censors quickly reduced it to a moralistic triviality. For years, *Pandora's
Box* was preserved only in incomplete versions held in European
archives and remained something of a legendary masterpiece. Then
the Cinémathèque Française in Paris and the Cinémathèque Suisse
in Lausanne gathered the extant prints and assembled a relatively
complete print following the plan of Pabst's shooting script. Fortunately for succeeding generations, this same print has recently been
acquired for American distribution, so that now after almost fifty
years audiences can once again experience the power and beauty of
Pabst's creation.

Pandora's Box is a testament to Pabst's cinematic skill and his
ability to explore the uncharted depths of Louise Brooks, who ap-

pears serious yet innocent, sensual yet honest with an ambivalence the screen had never before reflected. Her innocence masks a destructiveness that can only be overcome by an equally alluring destructive force—Jack the Ripper, and it is this cloak of innocence that renders her threatening to the public guardians of morality. Seen today in relatively enlightened times, and in view of Pabst's artistic discretion, it is remarkable that *Pandora's* subtle eroticism still retains its appeal. For Wedekind, Lulu's amorality symbolized a decline in bourgeois values, but for Pabst she became a liberated figure of pure untrammelled feminine desire.

Mountain Interlude: *Die Weisse Holle vom Pitz-Palü*

Pabst had planned as his next project the novel *Professor Unrat*, by his friend Heinrich Mann, presumably to feature his new discovery, Louise Brooks, in the role of Lola-Lola; but this was, of course, destined to be realized by Josef von Sternberg and Marlene Dietrich as the international success *Der Blaue Engel* (The Blue Angel) the following year.

While formulating plans to establish his own film company, Pabst agreed to co-direct a film with Dr. Arnold Fanck, a former geologist, who began in 1920 to produce a series of films devoted to the beauties and hazards of mountain climbing that soon developed into a distinctly Germanic film tradition with successes such as *Berg des Schicksals* (Peak of Destiny, 1924) and *Der Heilige Berg* (The Holy Mountain, 1927). These hybrid works were notable for their ravishingly beautiful photography of natural landscapes and, as Siegfried Kracauer points out, came to symbolize in their stereotyped situations a youthful, immature, heroic idealism:

These films were extraordinary in that they captured the most grandiose aspects of nature at a time when the German screen offered nothing but studio-made scenery. In subsequent films, Fanck grew more and more keen on combining precipices with passion, inaccessible steeps and human conflicts. . . . As documents these films were remarkable achievements . . . the glittering white of glaciers against a sky dark in contrast . . . the ice stalactites hanging down from roofs and windowsills of some small chalet, and inside crevasses, weird ice structures awakened to iridescent life by the torchlights of a nocturnal rescue party.[8]

Dr. Fanck's weakness lay in a lack of imagination in dealing with dramatic situations. Thus, Pabst was asked to concentrate his efforts

on all scenes in which "action" predominated, while Fanck was to
direct the documentary aspects of the film. Though far from a masterpiece, *Die Weisse Holle vom Pitz-Palü* was a notable improve-
ment over earlier and later efforts in the same vein of "mountain
genre." The story follows almost precisely the pattern of its predecessors, though Pabst's scenarist, Ladislaus Vajda, has given it a
more credible dramatic structure.

Dr. Johannes Krafft, who has lost his young bride in an avalanche
during an ascent of Mount Palü, returns there each year to honor
her memory. On this particular occasion, he meets fiancés, Maria
and Karl, who also plan to climb the dangerous peak despite Krafft's
story and his warnings. They join a group of students who scale the
mountain and who are swept away by a break in the ice and trapped
on a precipice for three days until spotted by an aviator. Krafft joins
the search party which following a spectacular avalanche, is only
able to save Maria and Karl. Petrified by his memory of the previous
tragedy, Krafft is himself killed.

Pabst evidently exerted considerable influence on the film, for his
knowledge of camera angles and the splendidly detailed photography of Sepp Allgeier, who was to join Pabst for his next production,
abound in contrasts, particularly in the avalanche sequences and the
flickering torchlight of the night search. Though Pabst tends to
restrain the actors and soft-pedal the melodrama, the scenes on the
precipice are marred by Leni Riefenstahl's overplaying, and the
neurosis inherent in Gustav Diessl's character barely achieves any
psychological depth. Leni Riefenstahl, who rose to prominence in
this genre and went on to direct *Das Blaue Licht* (The Blue Light),
an outstanding example of the type, later achieved notoriety as the
creator of the famous hymn to Nazism, *Triumph of the Will*. Pre-
dictably, *Pitz-Palü* in spite of its faults, became a tremendous financial success throughout the world and it was redistributed with a
recorded music score in 1935.

Social Realism: *Das Tagebuch einer Verlorenen*

The mixture of praise and outrage that greeted *Die Büchse der
Pandora* did not dissuade Pabst from establishing his own produc-
tion company and proceeding to undertake an even more provoca-
tive subject following his brief association with Dr. Arnold Fanck.
From a novel of Margarethe Boehme, Pabst and his scenarist Rudolf
Leonhardt (who had worked on *Jeanne Ney*) once again took up a

detailed and even more corrosive portrait of German society, whose corrupt bourgeoisie was soon to propel Hitler to power. United with this is a further exploration of the radical sexual freedom etched in *Pandora's Box* in his heroine, again portrayed by Louise Brooks. Pabst returns to the harsh, unglamorized imagery of *Die Freudlose Gasse*, but rejects the vocabulary of Expressionism to concentrate on the brutal, inhuman, gluttonous, and often erotic milieu. And for all its dramatic thrust, *Das Tagebuch einer Verlorenen* is equally a fictionalized documentary on the moral and social climate of Berlin in 1929. Like *Pandora's Box*, it was ruthlessly attacked by the press and censors, and ultimately Pabst was obliged to film an alternative ending (only for German audiences) that flagrantly reversed the irony of his work.

Structurally, the narrative is composed of three large distinct movements or sections, each roughly corresponding to a social aggregate as seen through the eyes of the heroine, Thymiane Henning, a pharmacist's daughter. The opening section details the atmosphere of the Henning household.

For an unexplained reason, Henning, a respectable pharmacist, dismisses his governess, Elizabeth. Sly close-ups of Meinert, his assistant, suggest there has been a liaison between him and the governess (an impression easily conveyed by Fritz Rasp's shifty eyes). From a floor-level angle, Pabst instantly exposes Meinert's suppressed desire for Thymiane by framing the supple movements of her legs. Fascinated by his direct advances, Thymiane initially controls her instincts, but later agrees to a rendezvous with him.

After her sixteenth birthday Thymiane celebrates her first communion. Among her gifts she receives a diary—to become one of her most treasured possessions—from her aunt, and a medallion with the family coat of arms from Count Osdorff. The festive occasion is interrupted by the discovery of Elizabeth's suicide. Pabst does not initially show the body, but in a detailed panoramic shot captures the individual reactions of the family and guests, revealing their heartless duplicity beneath shocked exteriors. Overwhelmed, Thymiane becomes hysterical and faints while ascending the staircase.

Later that evening as Meinert closes the pharmacy, Thymiane awakens, still clasping her diary, and goes to keep her appointment. Pabst builds up the mounting erotic attraction through alternating close shots, first through the shop door until she finally surrenders to his caresses against the closed door and falls sleepily into his arms. Rudolf Leonhardt, in a letter to historian Lotte Eisner (quoted in *The Haunted Screen*), recalls how the hand of the censor intervened here: "One copy shows the chemist's assistant giving Thymiane a kiss, and in the next image she is seen cuddling a baby./ I had a very beautiful scene: the girl faints and the assistant chemist takes her in his arms and carries her into the bedroom, her feet slipping over the display table; he lays her on her bed and her feet knock over a glass of red wine which spills over the bedcothes—a symbol for those who understand, a *Stimmungsbild* for the others."[9] (In the print which I viewed at the Murnau-Stifftung in Wiesbaden, the scene which Leonhardt describes was restored to its original context, though Thymiane's pregnancy and the birth of her child are left to the spectator's deduction.) This swift ellipsis is significant, however, since Pabst is more immediately concerned with the consequences of the sexual union and the reactions of the family to it. Shamed and dishonored, Henning insists that Meinert marry her, but he refuses on the grounds that the dowry will not be sufficient. Ironically, though he is the seducer, the family arrives at a collective decision to retain him and, to assuage the family honor, Thymiane is sent to a girl's reformatory. Henning agrees, though plainly distressed by the harsh measure because of his affection for Thymiane.

Scenes of the family life are employed as counterpoint to the hard, relentless realism of the middle section which takes place in the reformatory. The director, a bald, libidinous and totally hardened voyeur, is unforgettably portrayed by Andrews Englemann, who later became a significant figure in Nazi cinema. Equally memorable is Valeska Gert as his wife, a domineering, shrewish, and sadistic watchdog over the delinquent girls. She forces them to eat a tasteless broth to the timed beat of a metronomic wand, and later, for regimented calesthenics, Pabst shows her body rocking from side to side dictating the rhythm like a clock pendulum; with sadistic glee she moves faster and faster, then suddenly stops.

Into this atmosphere of severe disciplinarianism comes Thymiane, resisting at every turn attempts to force conformity to the rules. When she and her new friend Erika are caught applying lipstick by the director—makeup being forbidden—Pabst pursues a note of perverse psychology by lingering on the man brooding over the lipstick, then secretly applying it to his own mouth. He has just permitted Count Osdorff to visit Thymiane, and his sensual delight

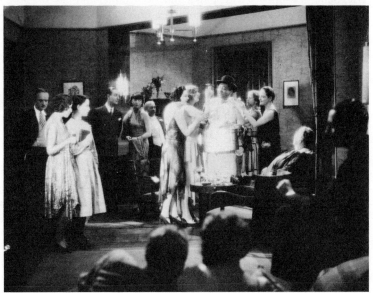

Reformatory and brothel scenes from Das Tagebuch einer Verlorenen

is intensified at catching a reflection of the two embracing in a hand mirror.

That evening, in the dormitory, Thymiane recounts their grievances over punishment exacted for the slightest infraction of the rules. The atmosphere of dissension and incipient revolt is sparked off when the director's wife tries forceably to take away Thymiane's diary. As the diary passes from one girl to another and back again, the camera darts back and forth in swift panning that builds the visual excitement to its climax when the girls descend *en masse* on their oppressors, and to the cadence of a gong, they act out their repressed hatred. Taking advantage of the disruption, Thymiane and Erika escape from the institution.

While Erika takes up with Count Osdorff, Thymiane goes to claim her child, who had been given to foster parents. Saddened, yet relieved, upon learning of the child's death, she wanders through the city, passing through progressively poorer quarters. An encounter with a street vendor leads her to a brothel, presided over by an apparently respectable, sweet, grandmotherly madame. Here Thymiane is reunited with Erika and the Count, and her presence in this jaded milieu elicits a genuine admiration for her timid gestures and unaffected beauty from men and women alike. Erika decides to let her wear her new dress, adding the final touch to Thymiane's magnetism as she drinks her first glass of champagne surrounded by admirers. Soon, like the others, she falls under the spell of alcohol and with a mild persuasion surrenders to the pleasure of love, arching her beautifully expressive neck in a gesture of sensual abandon. The camera tracks in rhythmic movements, imitating the music, as couples drift languidly from the dance floor into the adjoining bedrooms. Freddy Buache has rightly called Thymiane's seduction scene "one of the purest, the most iridescent, and the most ineffably magnificent in the cinema's collection of erotica."[10] Pabst's treatment of sexuality was undoubtedly shocking to film audiences in 1929, but its honesty and forthrightness are natural and spontaneous when compared with the deceptive and inhuman character of the Henning household or the hideous climate of the reformatory.

Thymiane's basic honesty is revealed in the following sequence in which she refuses to accept money from the customer with whom she has spent the night. She soon, however, learns to accept gracefully the role she is forced to play. In a crowded nightclub—again emanating a convivial Pabstian atmosphere—she is entertaining a group of lecherous gentlemen when spied by Henning, with his new wife and Meinert, all astonished at Thymiane who is perched on the bar, attempting to ward off the attentions of a fat man. She is equally perturbed, but her attempts to reach Henning in the crowd are thwarted, keeping them at a distance, symbolically suggesting their disparity in social standing.

With another narrative ellipsis, Pabst and Leonhardt again demonstrate that they are less interested in events themselves than in their consequences and resulting motives. Henning dies and Meinert, now owner of the pharmacy, seeks the favor of the widow and her children. Henning, however, leaves the largest part of his inheritance to Thymiane, who is consequently sought out by Count Osdorff, for whom wealth is of greater importance than social background. Reassured that his marriage proposal will be accepted, he immediately begins plans to build a new home with his wife's fortune.

At the chemist shop, Thymiane meets the widow of Henning and her two children and, touched by their poverty, gives them a portion of her inheritance. His pride and egoism stung to the core, Meinert is enraged by her action, and upon learning of Thymiane's generosity, the count commits suicide. The treatment of these melodramatic twists remains subtle and indirect, using images as suggestive, expressive signs rather than "action" coordinates.

At the cemetery, following the count's funeral, Thymiane is naturally unable to express grief for the death of a man she never loved, while the relatives and the unscrupulous Meinert show a feigned image of grief, affected for the occasion. Thymiane, however, responds to the sympathetic words of consolation from the elderly Osdorff who is charmed by her beauty. She becomes his companion and, in a brief scene at the beach, she delights in his affectionate, paternal admiration of her childlike playful gestures. Finally, they are married, and like Lulu, Thymiane finds a momentary happiness in the pleasure of wealth and social position. Then, an elderly countess induces the couple to join a charity group, and they are obliged to visit the scene of Thymiane's former detention. In spite of her finery she is recognized by the director though he declines to reveal what he knows of the past. When Erika is presented to the group as a particularly troublesome example of their problems, she seeks protection from her former friend, now the Countess Osdorff. Dis-

closing her past association with the girl, Thymiane soundly denounces the cruelty and hypocrisy of the administration, leaving the
culprits in stunned silence.

This moral reckoning, satisfying in its own right, was required by
the film's distributors for a general release in Germany. But Pabst
had hardly intended to satisfy the self-righteous values of the German middle class. He had created a radically different ending to
sting the faces of the establishment in which Thymiane herself becomes the mistress of a brothel, rejecting the comforts of society and
of money. "She opted for a frank alienation from society," writes
Freddy Buache, "as opposed to the illusory benevolence of theology
or humanitarianism; she refused the camouflage of sentimental re-
formism, and assuming its condition, she incarnated the certitude
that an all-pervading evil can only be answered by a total transformation of the world."[11] The radical posture of this concluding comment suggests that Pabst's revolutionary sentiments were real and
leads to his succeeding period of "social conclusiveness" in
Westfront 1918, *Dreigroschenoper*, and *Kameradschaft;* but at the
same time, his willingness to compromise with the alternate ending
suggests that pragmatic considerations were equally persuasive.

As a whole, *Diary of a Lost Girl* is more thematically and stylistically unified than *Pandora's Box*, though it shares none of the earlier
film's pictorial richness. With a sharp and disciplined sense of
realism, Pabst rigorously excludes the romantic and sentimental,
without sacrificing any of his feeling for atmosphere or his interest in
psychology. Limiting himself largely to tightly composed close angles, Pabst concentrates on the actors' faces rather than the settings,
which have a bleak, frequently austere quality. The fluid editing
pattern in Pabst's last silent film proves—although there are the
usual explanatory and dialogue titles—the expressive eloquence of a
then dying art, soon to be totally replaced by the "talkie." Never
again was Pabst able to achieve such a powerfully cynical view of the
society he knew so well, and no director during the silent period
equalled his ability to create scenes of sustained erotic intensity that
appeal to our aesthetic sense as well as our innermost desires.

Fritz Rasp's performance as the lascivious Meinert and the elec-
trifying characterizations of Andrews Engelmann and Valeska Gert
as the reformatory directors are still amazingly powerful, but it is
the glowing presence of Louise Brooks as Thymiane that holds our
attention, and her beauty is more natural and less manipulated than
in *Pandora's Box*. Here again on full display are the qualities that

Pabst found so appealing in her: the rapturous smile and personal charm, an impetuous, mercurial temperament, and a natural grace and intelligence in facial and body movements.

Reflecting on Miss Brooks's contribution to *Diary of a Lost Girl* for his 1955 exhibition, *60 Ans de Cinéma*, Henri Langlois, of the Cinémathèque Française, penned one of the most beautiful tributes ever made to a film actress.

Those who have seen her can never forget her. She is the modern actress par excellence because, like the statues of antiquity, she is outside of time . . . she has the naturalness that only primitives retain before the lens. . . . She is the intelligence of the cinematographic process, she is the most perfect incarnation of *photogénie*; she embodies in herself all that the cinema rediscovered in its last years of silence: complete naturalness and complete simplicity.[12]

The "Lost Years" of Louise Brooks

After so much praise, in retrospect, of the radiant beauty of Louise Brooks, we might well wonder why she apparently disappeared without a trace after starring in one other film, Augusto Genina's *Prix de Beauté*, in 1930.

James Card, curator of film at Eastman House in Rochester, must be given full credit for the rediscovery of the actress and our enlightenment about her after thirty years of obscurity and neglect. "Only Dostoevsky collaborating with Budd Schulberg could tell the story of Louise Brooks from 1930 to 1955," writes Card, who learned in 1955 that she had isolated herself in a dreary New York apartment where she had been for almost a decade.[13] In a letter to Card, she confesses that Pabst urged her to stay in Germany, learn the language and work there, but she refused. On the last day of filming for *Diary of a Lost Girl*, Pabst cornered her: "when . . . we were sitting having coffee alone at a little table, he told me that my rich friends (meaning all the Riviera crowd that he detested) would play with me and throw me away straight to hell. That the story of Lulu was *my* story. And I just sat there and glared at him. (And he came so near to being right that I shudder now a little, thinking of it.)"[14]

In 1930, back in New York, a former Follies friend, Peggy Fears, now married to a financier, came to Louise's aid and persuaded Columbia Pictures to offer her a $500-a-week contract. After waiting an hour in the outer office of Columbia, she left to keep another appointment without signing the contract. Forced to undergo numerous indignities in Hollywood as retribution, her refusal to submit to Harry Cohn's demand that she don a wig and play in a Buck Jones western finished her career in the movies, except for a brief appearance as a chorus girl in a Grace Moore musical after becoming disillusioned with night-club life in New York and returning to Hollywood desperate for work.

In January of 1943, Louise Brooks returned to New York where she worked in radio, publicity, and as a salesgirl until 1948. From then until around 1955, she secluded herself in a First Avenue apartment where she spent most of the time educating herself in literature, painting, and ultimately writing her memorable, incisive, and witty memoirs. Many of these have appeared in the British journal, *Sight and Sound* and in *Film Culture* and are proof of her spiritual resilience.

But the sad story of Louise Brooks has an unexpectedly happy ending. Thanks to James Card, who discovered not a frivolous, decadent Lulu, but an intellectually mature woman, she discovered, for the first time in her life, the art of the cinema. She had never even seen the two films she made for Pabst, having been brainwashed in Hollywood into not taking herself or the movies seriously. After viewing hundreds of films at Eastman House, she discovered a wealth of insight into the art of acting for film; and with the revival of her films by film archives and museums in Europe and America, she has emerged from her solitary, reflective life into a well-deserved limelight, recognized as the intuitive artist that she has always been. And thanks to the magic of photography and cinema, especially during her brief Pabst period, we have preserved an eternally youthful image of her for generations to come.

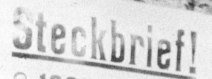

4

The Social Trilogy

The Aesthetics of Pacificism: *Westfront 1918*

BETWEEN 1930 AND 1931 Pabst directed in swift succession a trio
of films that brought him to the artistic summit of his career. The
first and last of these—*Westfront 1918* and *Kameradschaft*—
represent the strongest statement of his personal social and political
position and are the cornerstones of his frequently cited reputation
as a "realist," while *Dreigroschenoper* marks a return to his romantic,
quasi-Expressionist flair for visual textures and atmosphere. In each
of these films Pabst introduces, directly or implicity, some of the
themes dear to him: the transcendent value of love and friendship; a
distrust of capitalism, bourgeois values, and the establishment in
general; and a strong moral obligation to oppose the forces of armed
conflict. Even when these ideas appear overly optimistic for their
time, Pabst displays a tragic heroism, speaking out while others
were increasingly apathetic against the rising tide of fascism. The
fact that he managed to do so with such eloquence is significant; but
fortunately, for the sake of art and posterity, there remained more of
value in these works than Pabst's ideology.

By 1929, the revolutionary impact of the "talkie" was beginning to
be felt in Europe, and the Tobis Klangfilm recording system became standardized in its primitive form. Pabst travelled to London,
where E. A. Dupont, the celebrated German director of *Variety*,
had been invited to direct *Atlantic*, one of the first important British
sound films. There, Pabst, along with his old friend and former
associate Carl Froelich, studied the new production methods and
saw a number of early sound films from Hollywood. Like his con-
frères, Charles Chaplin and René Clair, both of whom he admired
enormously, Pabst instinctively felt that most of these pictures
merely exploited sound rather than used it as as an expressive ele-

75

Captain Rudolf Forster as Mack the Knife in Die Dreigroschenoper

ment in the production's total design. At the same time he realized that sound images would be a definite part of the future and encouraged his assistant, Marc Sorkin, in his directorial debut to make a talking film.

Pabst's own first attempts at the new medium proved him as sensitive to the expressive possibilities of sound as well as image. Nevertheless, his faith in the plastic essence of film remained strong, as evidenced in an essay from 1937. "In spite of the rise of the 'talkie' I remain convinced that in the cinema, the text counts for little. What counts is the image. So I would still claim that the creator of a film is much more the director than the author of the scenario or the actors."[1] Though he occasionally lapses into silent film techniques and often minimizes the importance of spoken dialogue, the early experiments with sound in these films remain impressive in spite of their technical crudeness.

Returning to Germany in the spring of 1930, Pabst began work with Ladislaus Vajda on a screen version of Ernst Johannsen's novel, *Vier von der Infanterie*, which described the experiences during the Great War of four infantry soldiers from slightly different social backgrounds. Pabst and Vajda decided to break away from the prevailing conventions of narrative melodrama and adopt a detached, freer thematic approach, allowing for contrasts in development while avoiding any concessions to sentimentality.

The tradition of the war film from Griffith's *Hearts of the World* (1919) and King Vidor's *The Big Parade*, (1925) to Lewis Milestone's *All Quiet on the Western Front* (1930) and even Jean Renoir's later *La Grande Illusion* (1938), was to follow the pattern of dramatizing and sentimentalizing the experience of war to produce a highly charged emotional response. Pabst, on the other hand, wished to de-dramatize war in order to expose it for what it is: the most horrible of human follies. By tracing typical wartime experiences of four men through a dispassionate and nonrhetorical statement of incident, *Westfront* captures the ebb and flow of existence in the dugouts and trenches, alternating moments of surreal horror with ennui, camaraderie with courtship and marital conflicts.

The initial image is that of fraternity, a moment of release from the pressures of combat in which some German soldiers are enjoying themselves at a French tavern. The fraternalism of Germans and Frenchmen, which finds its fullest expression in *Kameradschaft*, is focused in the character of the idealistic young student (Hans Joachim Moebis), fresh from the university, who experiences his first night of idyllic love with Yvette, a tavern maid. However, this deceptive, lyrical mood is swept away by the sounds of an air raid, dissolving into the march to the front and the introduction of Karl (Gustav Diessl), a young engineer.

The approach to the front at dawn is treated like a large newsreel tableau. The camera tracks relentlessly along the desolate lunar landscape, encompassing a succession of seemingly random details, part of an aesthetically designed, yet realistic appearing pattern: piles of corpses, mazes of barbed wire, ruined buildings jutting out of the smoldering atmosphere. Eschewing his former method of detailed close angles and editing, Pabst refrains from any overt symbolic commentary, letting landscapes and objects merge into a continuous, natural design. Here, at least, he seems closer to the goals of *Neue Sachlichkeit* than in any previous film.

The realism of *mise-en-scène* is enhanced by the detailed, yet entirely unforced and credible performances of the young soldiers, whose collective and separate experiences give structural unity to the story. Claus Clausen, as the lieutenant, reflects the Spartan idealism of a military aristocracy, completely devoted to the Kaiser and the fighting cause. The resourceful Gustav Diessl in the role of Karl provides a nuanced interpretation of a typical youth, torn from the ties of marriage and profession, in an absurd conflict. Fighting shoulder to shoulder with him is Fritz Kampers, as a Bavarian peasant whose cheerfulness and adaptability to rigorous conditions relieves the unbearable tension for the others and for the spectator as well. And rounding off the quartet is the inexperienced young student who undertakes a mission behind enemy lines to be reunited with his sweetheart.

Almost every early sound film included a song or "specialty number"—usually for its own sake and unrelated to the action. Pabst includes similar sequences to indicate lulls in the combat at the front: a band performing a military march and a clown and violinist doing a vaudeville routine for the troops in an assembly hall. Later, he films Kampers accompanied by a soldier's harmonica singing a Bavarian folk song at an increasingly rapid tempo, just prior to an artillery assault. Owing to the technical requirements of recording the actual sound while filming, the camera remains in a fixed position throughout, yet the visual invention within the frame and off-screen sound environment lift these scenes totally out of the category of show-stoppers; further, and more importantly, they are firmly integrated into the film's total design.

Gustav Diessl in trench and church scenes from Westfront 1918

When Karl obtains leave to visit his wife in Hamburg, Pabst suggests, with a few brief and well-chosen scenes, the demoralized condition of German society he earlier detailed in less realistic terms in *Die Freudlose Gasse*. In a long and depressing food queue, Karl's mother is overcome at learning of her son's return from the battlefield. The reunion of mother and soldier, an emotion-filled scene found in virtually every war film, is here the foreground to a greater passing irony. As Karl makes his way through the streets, a band of recruits marches off to the front, and the crowd's patriotic cheers and applause are a counterpoint to the mother's tears.

Karl's eagerness to surprise his wife is short-lived when he finds her in bed with the butcher's son. As the threatened and cowering boy leaves the room, the admonished young wife exclaims, "But you were gone such a long time!" The arrival of Karl's mother—beautifully characterized by Else Heller—brings about their temporary reconciliation. Older and more understanding of such things, she blames the wife's affair not so much on her son's absence as on the more encompassing evil of war, disrupting the natural unity of things. Karl, however, proves unable to forgive his wife, and their emotional isolation is made clear by long periods of silence in which he refuses to speak with her. Throughout, Pabst maintains a distance from the actors and, rather than break up the visual field by editing, has Fritz Arno Wagner (who also photographed his next three films) maintain a fluid, mobile camera that gives the images a vibrant immediacy and detailed realism.

The final section opens on a quiet retreat from battle at the front with the Bavarian singing of home, as the peace is abruptly shattered by a barrage of artillery fire. Following a tearful parting from his sweetheart, Yvette, the student returns across enemy lines to join his regiment but meets sudden death in hand-to-hand combat with a Frenchman. Pabst does not linger on the struggle but moves to a discreet distance from the dugout, denying us the sort of heart-rending poetics that Milestone (*All Quiet on the Western Front*) or King Vidor (*The Big Parade*) extract from similar scenes. Meanwhile, back in the city, Karl, still stung by his wife's infidelity, leaves home without saying farewell. At the front, he affects his former cheerfulness, but the cries of the wounded Frenchman who killed his young comrade in the dugout renew his anger and remorse.

In the concluding sequence, Pabst brings to bear all his skill in imagery and sound to build tempo and visual tension as the lieutenant's company is virtually annihilated by the French. The battlefield is transformed into a bloody landscape of death, a surreal nightmare reflected on the traumatized face of the shell-shocked lieutenant as he wanders through corpse-strewn trenches. He is transported to a bombed church, which has been converted into a temporary hospital; there the camera travels past scores of wounded to the operating room, while choruses of agony provide a background to the lieutenant's delirious screams.

Fatally wounded, Karl is placed on a pallet next to a wounded Frenchman, where, in a moment of feverish hallucination, he forgives his wife and is assured of her love. In the final moments, Pabst must have recalled Severin Mars' anguished demise at the conclusion of Abel Gance's powerful anti-war film, *J'Accuse* (1919). Karl's death is rendered by the extinguishing of a light so that his eyes, remaining open, have the horrifying impression of two gaping holes. The wounded Frenchman, unaware that he has expired, reaches to grasp the dead man's hand, murmuring, "Moi, camarade. Pas ennemi." A final note of irony is found in the closing title's question mark: "Ende?" suggesting Pabst's pessimism for the future in spite of his fervent pacificism.

Westfront was premiered on May 23, 1930 at the Capitol Theatre in Berlin. Although acknowledging Pabst's artistry, the press found little to praise in a work that so graphically showed German military defeat, especially at a time when the country was already primed for another war for the Fatherland. In his later historical study, Kracauer finds the film lacking in that it sidesteps the issues of war and sociopolitical polarization in Germany. Not satisfied with a work of art with a tone of social protest, he seems to advocate more overtly political propaganda, as is clear in his conclusion that *Westfront's* "fundamental weakness consists in not transgressing the limits of pacificism itself. The film tends to demonstrate that war is intrinsically senseless and monstrous."[2] Precisely. But this *a priori* critique fails to take into account that the polarization of forces had reached such a point by 1930 that an overtly anti-military, not to mention anti-war statement would hardly have survived the gauntlet of German censors, and Kracauer fails to mention that only two years later, on April 27, 1933, *Westfront*, like subsequent Pabst films, was banned by the *Filmprufstelle*.

In France, as well as in England, *Westfront* was highly regarded by critics, though some, like Jean Paul Dreyfus and Jean-Georges

Auriol in *La revue du cinéma,* while admiring Pabst's pacifism found it less effective than Milestone's *All Quiet on the Western Front,* in its lack of emotional appeal that could move and "convert" apathetic spectators. (Apparently, they were unaware that at least twenty spectators fainted at the Berlin première.) Seen today, however, the authentically moving moments in Milestone's film—more a Hollywood product than a personally felt work—are few. Although it too deals with a German youth's realization of the horrors of war, its all-American cast headed by Louis Wolheim, Lew Ayres, and Raymond Griffith, and theatrically arch dialogue compare poorly with Pabst's less ostentatious, but more genuine work. Although he was not directly involved in the war, Pabst was interred in a prisoner-of-war camp during the war as an enemy alien and his experiences there left an indelible mark on him that must have found an outlet in *Westfront.*

In his analysis of camera movements, the influential French critic André Bazin has theorized that the use of tracking and panning shots to capture a continuous scene or action renders it more realistically than a traditional breakdown into long, close, and medium shots. Pabst's reunion with Fritz Arno Wagner, who had begun exploring the possibilities of this technique in *Jeanne Ney,* allowed him to devise methods of moving the camera most effectively in conjunction with Ernö Metzner's carefully designed sets, while using the soundtrack to imaginative ends.

In 1930, the technique of mixing sound from various sources onto one track did not yet exist. Sound effects and dialogue were recorded together and there was no way of varying the sound volume. Consequently, the sound of artillery bombardment had to be eliminated to insert lines of dialogue. As Pabst's assistant, Paul Falkenberg, recalled, this crude method required numerous painstaking trials and errors before an acceptable syncronization could be achieved. Thus, relying chiefly on the expressiveness of the image to carry the principal impact, Pabst depended on an impressionistic sound that amplifies rather than duplicates the camera's realism. The complexity of overlapping sound in the final hospital scene is still astonishing enough to be placed in an anthology of early aural accomplishments, along with Lang's use of ambient sound in *M* and Sternberg's use of sound dissolves in *Der Blaue Engel.*

In an age where atrocities have become almost commonplace and our sensibilities are numbed to the suffering of war by ultra-violent battle epics, *Westfront* may seem too remote and fastidious for some. Yet, its dispassionate, stylized, realistic vision retains the imaginative force of a searing protest of the self-defeating, absurd theater of war.

Frivolous Interlude: *Skandal um Eva*

Prior to beginning his next major work, Pabst directed a light comedy-drama, *Skandal um Eva*, with the popular German actress, Henny Porten, who had starred in his early silent production, *Gräfin Donelli*. The assignment was undertaken as a favor to Pabst's friend and producer, Seymour Nebenzahl, whose company (Nero Films) accorded Pabst an unprecedented freedom in his most important early sound films. As with *Gräfin Donelli*, Pabst was presented with a finished script, a pre-determined cast and crew and was simply required to put them through their paces. The inconsequential plot concerned a schoolmistress who becomes engaged to the local minister of education, only to discover the day after that he already has a four-year-old son.

Surprisingly, everyone concerned was quite pleased with the results. It was Henny Porten's first sound film and she apparently handled the dialogue with considerable grace. Although it was strictly a commercial confection over which Pabst had no personal control, he was surprised to find that he was able to direct a successful light comedy, and in only fifteen days.

Skandal um Eva proved a great financial success, though admiring critics of Pabst were shocked to find his name associated with this *divertissement* following the somber realism of *Westfront*. *Close Up*, whose staff held Pabst in high regard, published a brief, anonymous notice:

. . . One moment at the beginning is excellent: classrooms, the elderly schoolmistress controlling a restive but respectful class, the recitation of a poem by Heine by nervous fumbling schoolchildren to the inspector. But from then on we are taken on a picnic in order that Henny Porten may sing to her pupils, we are then introduced to a four-year-old child so that we may note his first attempts to sing to a musical box and then his chase throughout the rest of the film of the schoolmistress, to whom he must cry "Mama" thereby causing scandal.[3]

Strangely, as is true of *Gräfin Donelli,* no prints of the film seem to have survived, though a copy of the shooting script has been preserved by the Museum of Modern Art in New York. Its loss is undoubtedly slight, but its comic atmosphere must have prepared Pabst for another popular subject that captured his imagination for more serious and personal reasons.

Pabst Interprets Brecht: *Die Dreigroschenoper*

Pabst's cinematic treatment of Bertolt Brecht and Kurt Weill's well-known *Dreigroschenoper* provides us with a key to the analogy comparing Pabst to the romantic conductor-interpreter. Though he was never noted for temperament, Pabst clearly believed that the original material for a film, be it a novel or play, was simply a framework, a ground plan that would eventually be transformed to suit his own preoccupations and visual imagination; thus his work involved creation rather than adaptation.

The immediate subject at hand by Brecht and Weill was an elaboration on John Gay's famous eighteenth century satire, *The Beggar's Opera,* written in 1728. Gay (1685–1732) was a poet and playwright who would have remained relatively obscure if he had not been inspired by Swift to burlesque the English pastoral tradition at a moment when Italian opera was making popular inroads into England. Numerous artists and intellectuals of the time found this florid operatic style, employing castrati singers, effete and an unhealthy influence. As a counterbalance to this phenomenon, Gay's ballad opera, using well-known English ballad airs, satirized the court circle by comparing it to the underworld. It became a phenomenal success and ran for years, bringing its author riches and fame. His Macheath, based on an actual outlaw figure of the day, was a supreme romantic hero, not unlike Robin Hood, a defender of the oppressed beggars exploited by Peachum, but who rises to a social position by an equally immoral system of thievery.

Two hundred years later, in 1928, when Brecht and Weill's version opened in Berlin, it made them an overnight success as well. Although the Theater am Schiffbauerdamm production was carried out strictly according to Brecht's directions, it would be a mistake to assume that critics or audiences were captivated by Brecht's bitter cynicism about the human condition. Rather, they were taken with Kurt Weill's jazz-influenced, easily singable score and songs, such as "Mack the Knife," and "The Pirate's Song," which soon became popular hits. The production's merits tended, in fact, to obscure its weakness from a political viewpoint. Brecht's text, which he hoped would be ironically underscored by the dry, staccato delivery of the singers and by didactic placards spelling out revolutionary slogans, failed, for all its Expressionist devices and distancing effects, to provide a recognizable antithesis to the immoral system of values advocated by Macheath and his gang of thieves.

"In adapting the cynical romantic pose of their predecessors," writes German critic Walter Weideli, "Brecht and Weill, far from attacking the social conflicts of their own time, were creating a misunderstanding which had to turn, out of necessity, against their naively revolutionary intentions. They intended to denounce the hypocrisy and resignation of the lower middle class, but the public saw in their songs only a secret complicity."[4]

Pabst agreed to direct the film version as he was in sympathy with Brecht's political and social ideas and he was undoubtedly sensitive to the "secret complicity" sensed by audiences that made the stage version so popular and thereby acceptable to the authorities. This may account for the deletion of numerous songs and alterations made during filming.

Leo Lania, who was responsible for making the first treatment in collaboration with Brecht, recalls the conditions of the agreement.

When *Dreigroschenoper* was sold to Warner Brothers, Brecht stipulated in the contract that nothing from the original stage version must be changed. Since changes were unavoidable in a motion picture adaptation, he decided that since he couldn't—he wouldn't aspire to knowing, or to deciding what those changes would have to be—that I should have the last word, and that I should do the screen adaptation and at the same time act as his advisor and as the man he trusted most. He knew that I spoke, as it were, his language as far as theatre was concerned, and at the same time I had had experience in motion pictures. Pabst was most happy about the arrangement, knowing it would be difficult to work with Brecht anyhow. . . .[5]

Lotte Eisner reports, however, that from the very first there were conflicting ideas about the general conception to be followed in the treatment. Brecht's approach was analytic, breaking the action into brief episodes, interrupted by the caustic and melancholy melodies of Kurt Weill. Since he had written the play in 1928, Brecht's social views had become broadened from sympathy for the proletariat's oppression to specific Marxism and he insisted on a sharper satire of the materialism of a repressive, bougeois capitalism. The outline of his new revision, entitled *The Boss,* has been published by *Cahiers du cinéma* (No. 114, December 1960). This revision, which would have had immense appeal to a director like Sergei Eisenstein, or even more to the contemporary French director Jean-Luc Godard, was not at all what Pabst had in mind. He wanted a smoother, more classical continuity, embellished by a more colorful interpretation of the Victorian period, as opposed to the eighteenth century; and he insisted on placing the songs at points where they would not break up the dramatic action. Neither was he apparently in sympathy with the new character of "The Boss," an authoritarian figure who was to suppress the lower classes and become the focus of attention in the people's revolt. The inability to compromise points of view led to an impasse and ultimately a new screenplay written by Ladislaus Vajda and the Hungarian journalist-critic Bela Balàsz. While Pabst had already begun shooting what was to be one of his most ambitious and successful films, Brecht and Weill launched one of the liveliest lawsuits in the history of cinema.

According to Lotte Eisner, "Brecht was profoundly shocked by Pabst's transposition, which he saw as an intolerable adulteration of the ideological and stylistic content of his play."[6] Brecht and Weill brought proceedings against Nero Films in Berlin, asking for the production of the film to cease on the grounds of their copyright. When confronted with the challenge that he had appropriated other authors' copyrights—in particular, the translation of lyrics by Villon—Brecht retorted that he had acknowledged an agreement with the author and further asserted that he was not simply defending his literary work, but rather "the property of the spectator." That is, Brecht felt the spectator should in some way be assured that the author's work was being transmitted according to his intentions, as if cinema were merely a mechanical vehicle for the transmission of his play. Ultimately, Brecht's plea was turned down on grounds that he had not honored the terms of his contract and had willfully ended his collaboration on the screen treatment. Weill, who, unlike Brecht, had continued working with the producers until dismissed by them, pursued and won his case.

Pabst himself took no part in the controversial court action, but continued shooting, modifying, and even improvising on the text. The film was lavishly budgeted with the financial assistance of Tobis and Warner Brothers, provided on the basis of the play's reputation and the popularity of its songs. To ensure an even wider distribution, a French version was made simultaneously, employing a largely alternate cast. While he respected Brecht and Weill's work, Pabst felt the radical revision that had been proposed would not make a successful film, artistically or financially, and with so much at stake in the production, he felt more inclined to trust the instincts of his writers, Lania, Vajda and Balàsz. Furthermore, he must have seen in it the possibility of crystallizing themes and atmospheric motifs explored in his earlier work. His strain of humanism and love of detailed *mise-en-scène* could not mesh well with the pithy schematics and dry, critical tone of Brecht.

The major change in the emphasis of dramatic action shows that while he sympathizes with the play's social thesis, Pabst is more intimately concerned with the characters and the sentiments that unite them. The central force that galvanizes the film is the love of Mack, the leader of the underworld gang, and Polly Peachum, daughter of the King of the Beggars, a relationship treated only incidentally in Brecht's play. The principal conflict is engendered by Peachum's bitter opposition to the alliance and his plotting with "Tiger" Brown, the corrupt police commissioner and Mack's former comrade-at-arms in India, to keep the lovers apart. This bittersweet elaboration goes, however, beyond the level of fantasy and romantic melodrama. Underlying the melodious poetry of mocking thievery and thwarted love is the sinister corruption of Brecht's world, reflected in the shadowy surfaces of Fritz Arno Wagner's exquisite photography and the multileveled architectural environment of dark alleys, hanging rigging, and stairways created by Pabst's gifted designer, Andrei Andreiev.

Pabst's film opens with Mack and Jenny, his current flame, parting on the docks of London, in a setting that is clothed, as Lotte Eisner has beautifully observed, "in chiaroscuro and mist, making the brick walls of the Thames-side docks and Soho slums both real and fantastic at the same time."[7] Amidst a series of painted backdrops and artificial props, the crowd of beggars and poor folk appear like animated figures in a landscape. During his introduction by the Strassensänger [Street-Singer]—whose role as Brecht's choral commentator is considerably reduced in the film—with "The Ballad of Mack the Knife," Mackie leaves Jenny to stroll through the streets. A series of fluid, lengthy tracking shots follows Rudolf Forster's supple, arrogant, self-confident survey of the byways of his Soho turf, while the Strassensänger's verses illustrated by crudely painted designs suggest he is a notorious murderer and robber. (While the sets remain true to the rendering of English street signs, as the film progresses, Pabst takes the liberty of using German for important passages; the same substitution occurs in the French version.) The respectably dressed Mackie is arrested by the sight of Polly and Mrs. Peachum admiring a bridal costume in a shop window. Pabst creates a magic moment as Mack and Polly first meet each other's gaze through their reflections in the window, suggesting at once their magnetic attraction and imminent courtship.

Mack invites Polly and her mother to join him at the pub in the Cuttlefish Hotel where Jenny is refused entrance while Mack escorts the ladies into the tavern, filled with smoke, animated dancers, and convivial types. Although the shooting script provides for conversation between Mack and his gang concerning instructions for the planned wedding, these are abbreviated or eliminated entirely. Here, as elsewhere, Pabst reduces dialogue to silent screen standards concentrating on expressive gesture and atmospheric detail. While Jenny argues with the hotel doorman who has been instructed to keep her out, Pabst films Mack's proposal to Polly through a glass window partition, reducing their speech to mute pantomime. Mack's orders to the gang are delivered as unheard whispers and when he gives a written message to be "delivered" to Inspector Brown, it is passed from hand to hand, each registering a shocked reaction that reminds us of an American silent comedy.

The gang's nocturnal plundering of shops and department stores in preparation for the wedding, set only to music and isolated sound effects, evinces the choreographed grace and charm of an early René Clair film, especially the removal of a Chippendale grandfather clock from a shop with the aid of a uniformed bobby. Then, with the sound of a burglar alarm, the police descend on them and provide a splendid chase.

Mack and Polly's growing sentiments are given form in a "Love Duet," sung on a studio-moored vessel against an artificial backdrop, while Mat the Mint conveniently allows the police to capture him. Upon recognizing him, "Tiger" Brown orders his

Two wedding scenes from Die Dreigroschenoper. *Carola Neher celebrates her marriage to Mackie.*

officers out, blusteringly receives the message from Mackie, then ushers Mat out the back door, thus establishing his complicity with the gang.

The scene of the wedding has been changed from the stables of the Duke of Devonshire to a riverside warehouse where a tapestry-curtain is raised to reveal a shimmering array of food and dinner-ware on an immense table bathed in candlelight, surrounded by Polly's recently acquired wedding trophies. The gang prepares a lavish setting for the arrival of the lovers accompanied by song and dance, while two offer a parody of the bride and groom gazing at themselves in a mirror. The arrival of Mack and Polly has a quieting effect on the boisterous gang and though many of their comments have been omitted, Mack's supercilious denunciation of the loot as "junk" has been retained, revealing his affected regard for finery. With the arrival of "Tiger" Brown, a frightened pastor performs the nuptial rites—without a word spoken. Here Pabst and Fritz Arno Wagner revel in *clair-obscur*: the wedding chandeliers, candlea-bras, plates, carpets, along with bodies and faces are radiant, or-dered around the pivotal theme of Polly's iridescent white wedding dress. Following the wedding feast, Polly's song—"Barbara" not "Pirate Jenny" as indicated in the original script—offered as enter-tainment for the guests, tells of her disinterest in nice, moneyed, respectable suitors and her inclination toward men who make their romantic intentions clear from the beginning. Although the camera remains passive, in close shot, for the duration of the song, Carola Neher's crisp delivery and animated gestures, surrounded by the glow of her wedding costume, are so enchanting that all else is temporarily relegated to the background. "I like the words, very nice," responds one of the gang, to which Mack tartly retorts, "Nice! It's not nice, it's art, you fool!" pointing up his bourgeois pretenti-ousness and at the same time his failure to appreciate the feminine sentiment expressed in the song. This remark also foreshadows the ironic turn of events in that money, not love, is the force that ultimately unites the two.

Whereas the stunning wedding sequence is a brilliant display of impressionistic light values, the world of the beggars, lorded over by the totally unscrupulous Jeremiah Peachum, is created with clas-sic Expressionist idioms. The walls of his residence—also his place of business—are laden with placards appealing to bourgeois senti-ments in homilies and biblical passages: "Do not turn a deaf ear to misfortune," or "Give and thou shalt be given." Beggars' costumes appear frozen into contorted positions, casting menacing shadows on the wall, and a beggar, arriving from the street with his earnings, suddenly "loses" his blindness and deformity upon entering the establishment. Peachum rationalizes his organized duplicity, making his livelihood by licensing and providing "props" for the poor to rob the rich, while he and his wife are heartlessly cruel and parsimonious in exploiting their class. (Fritz Rasp, otherwise perfect for the role of Peachum, unfortunately possessed no aptitude for singing, and since dubbing was a technical impossibility at the time, Peachum's "Morning Anthem" and other songs are omitted.) In his own way, an underworld demagogue and rival of Mackie Messer, Peachum is disturbed when Polly returns home and reveals her clandestine elopement, which will neither enrich the family nor elevate their status in society. On the stage Polly's defense to her parents is framed in the song, "Barbara," but Pabst has her state quite simply that "love is the most important thing in the world." In addition, the screenwriters have created a new scene in which Mr. and Mrs. Peachum go to Inspector Brown's office and threaten to disrupt the impending Coronation parade unless he has Mackie arrested and hanged, showing their determination to keep the lovers apart and the ambivalent loyalty of the police inspector to equally corrupt factions.

Paralleling this scene, Pabst introduces Mack, at his waterfront hideout, dictating plans for a robbery during the Coronation parade. He wants to move from petty thievery in the Soho to the big time. Jenny, his former lover, arrives with protestations of her love, but Mack lyrically expands on his feelings for Polly. Pabst films their initial encounter off-screen, with their figures blocked by a huge barrel; their tearful farewell is staged around an imposing staircase, recalling a similar structure in the final sequence of *Pandora's Box*, but here a symbolic link between the underworld and that of middle-class respectability.

Mack's departure to seek refuge from the law and his farewell to Polly are also staged on the same stairway. He transfers the command to his wife whose sweet, sentimental posture is suddenly transformed as she takes on the sharp, arrogant character of Mackie and slaps the face of a gang member when he infers that a woman could not do Mackie's job.

Jenny's betrayal of Mack is foreshadowed when he is ironically amused at a sign posting reward for his capture as Pabst cuts to a shot of Jenny, seen through a window at the brothel, placing money in her garter. Mack is welcomed with the pomp of a general into the lush, *fin de siècle* atmosphere of the brothel by a horde of chattering prostitutes, while Jenny sings "The Ballad of the Ship with Fifty Cannon" (substituted for the original "Tango Ballad"), suggesting her revenge for his betrayal of her affections. Mackie effects a reconciliation just in time to be warned of the police and adroitly evades his pursuers on the rooftops. The beautifully choreographed maneuvers have a stylistic resemblance—emphasized in the French version by Albert Préjean—again to René Clair. But the momentary allure of a streetwalker detains Mack long enough for Brown's men to move in for the capture.

The Strassensänger intervenes to sum up the moral of the action and to introduce us to the radically new environment of Mackie's "shrewd and loving wife." In Mackie's absence, Polly—as in Brecht's revised scenario—realizes she can make more money through a legitimate enterprise (that is, capitalism) than by the illegal activities of Mack's gang and follows in her father's footsteps to become singlehandedly a banker with the gang members as her board of directors. The spacious, geometrical, exaggerated architecture of her bank office immediately suggests the inflated comfort and security of a capitalist. Like all her bogus "directors," who instantly reveal their origins by their crass behavior, Polly is dressed in a business suit, but her aggressive, managerial tone is that of a leader. She orders bank funds to be sent to Brown to cover Mack's bail.

Meanwhile Peachum, unaware that Mackie has been arrested, and preparing his beggar forces for a demonstration speaks with the fervor of a real social revolutionist: "I discovered that the rich can't face the misery they make. They've got cold hearts but weak nerves. . . . We'll tear their nerves with all our power. . . . Don't be afraid, gentlemen, the Queen won't tolerate bayonets against cripples!" Suddenly Mrs. Peachum rushes in with the news that Mack has been arrested, but having roused the mob against their oppressors, Peachum is powerless to stop them. Parker Tyler describes the procession as "one of those alternately electric and lava-like social eruptions so graphically put forth in *Metropolis* but here suggestively realistic; like others, Peachum is ruined by the very underground power he had controlled and set in motion."[8] Intercut with this social upheaval is Mack's escape from jail, treated as a comic diversion. While Smith, the jailer—a brief cameo by Vladimir Sokoloff—prepares to serve Mackie his last meal, the repentant Jenny arrives to see him. With tears and a sly seductive smile, she diverts the jailer, allowing Mack the opportunity to escape, virtually unnoticed. At the same time, Brown in his office is disturbed by a report of the demonstration, and when the bank employee arrives with Mackie's bail and he phones for his release only to learn he has escaped, the inspector surrenders to apoplexy.

The march on Piccadilly provides fine material for the film's visual climax, contrasting agitated swirls of mass movement, placards everywhere protesting aristocratic wealth and the police who protect their power, with the stately, regimented movement of the Queen and her Royal Guard. As the royal procession is halted by the dramatic intersection with the stream of beggars, the Queen's face expresses shock at confronting the misery of her subjects and her patronizing gaze tends to disperse the concerted force of the beggars. It has been argued that the failure of the demonstrators proves that Pabst is not in sympathy with their revolt; however, even within the context of a musical fantasy, Pabst's realist sensibility would not conceive of a facile, optimistic victory. Writing about the film upon its American release in 1933, Harry Alan Potamkin, who was elsewhere extremely harsh in his ideological criticism of Pabst, puts the sequence in its proper perspective:

This is not a revolutionary assertion simply because it is not asserted by a revolutionary group and is not spoken in revolutionary terms. Still, in its undertones of vibrant social sympathy and its overtones sardonic in their satire, the picture transforms the raw material of *melodram*—in its original sense—into a very stirring approximation of the revolutionary march—an approximation that is not triumphant, as it could not be, but which is warm and in the direction of the element to which the victory belongs, as the film itself unquestionably leaves one to feel. The victory is Pabst's and it is a further step in his progress toward social conclusiveness.[9]

The epilogue, a creation of the screenwriters, follows the social polemic advocated by Brecht. "Tiger" Brown, now frightened and disgraced, and the beaten Peachum, join Mackie and Polly at the bank and agree to form a partnership in the concern. Mackie and Brown drink to their loyalty and sing "The Song of the Heavy Cannon," recalling their army days in India, while Polly is reconciled

Two scenes from Die Dreigroschenoper. *Top: G. W. Pabst directs Rudolf Forster in the cafe scene. Bottom: The Beggars' march on Picadilly.*

with her father. The scene's surface tone of camaraderie ends, however, with an ironic exchange between Peachum and his partners
outlining the logic of capitalism and big business that Brecht
strongly denounced.

"Only today did I understand the strength of poverty."

"But if the beggars are as powerful as you say, why do they need
us?"

"Because, they know that we need them."

Thus, the basis of an even greater and more efficient repressive
force is born, and the revolutionary struggle will only succeed
through a long series of protests of which this is only the beginning.
The crowd will disperse without its leaders, just as Brown's horse,
lost without its master, wanders aimlessly down a deserted, misty
street. At the same time, as Siegfried Kracauer has demonstrated,
this union of capital and labor, of establishment and underground,
sows the seeds of its own corruption, paving the way for a police
state. Therein lies the irony of the Strassensänger's final song: "The
revolt has returned to the shadows, the night will conceal it there
for a long time."

Pabst's film premiered in Berlin on February 19, 1931 and was
received with warmth and enthusiasm by the press, if not by government officials. Even though muted by Pabst's atmosphere and
his attempt to humanize the characters, the social and economic
problems of the Victorian era were soon exposed as a veiled criticism of contemporary Germany. The beginnings of political censor-
ship in the arts were felt when the German version was banned in
August 1933 by the *Filmprufstelle*. Meanwhile, the French version
drew large crowds and was acclaimed a masterpiece in Paris, while a
shortened version enjoyed a successful engagement in New York
and London.

Although the original negative of the German version of *Dreigroschenoper* was apparently destroyed by the Nazis, prints survived in several European countries, though none were complete.
After the war these prints were gathered and a complete version
was assembled which is currently in circulation. These faded copies,
so far removed from the lustrous, crisp black and white contrasts of
the original, make it difficult to judge the work's visual quality; and
by contemporary standards, the soundtrack seems archaic owing to
the difficulties of recording music and dialogue, often simultaneously.

Lotte Eisner's rapturous praise of the film, based on memories of the original Berlin showing and many subsequent viewings, echoes Paul Rotha's unqualified appreciation first published in *Celluloid* in 1933. If we look at more recent assessments, however, we find a more balanced, if at times equivocal, critical evaluation of Pabst's work. British critic, Alan Stanbrook, in a lengthy analysis in *Films and Filming*, concludes that "despite the many virtues of *Dreigroschenoper*, they are somehow never unified and remain isolated fragments. The film is finally a curio, though from an academic point of view it is often rewarding and tells us much about its director's range and limitations."[10] In her 1960 evaluation in *Film Quarterly*, American writer Arlene Croce—probably influenced by the special "Brecht et le cinéma" issue of *Cahiers du cinéma* (No. 114, December 1960) which included Brecht's original scenario—argues that although the film version underscores Brecht's ideas, it fails to develop a cinematic correlative for a Brechtian aesthetic and she takes the filmmakers to task for eliminating many of Weill's songs.

Pabst's film is, of course, not in any sense a Brechtian operetta and its elegant, stylish surfaces are far from the tawdry, plebeian ambience of cabaret theatre. If we go to the film expecting the latter, along with the missing songs (Mrs. Peachum's "Ballad of Sexual Dependency," "The Tango Ballad," Macheath's jail song, and "The Ballad of the Hangman," etc.), we are bound to be disappointed. Croce, unfortunately, sees in the screen version a "semi-theatricalized adaptation" which "is ultimately as fatal to Brecht as it is foreign to Pabst." "Pabst's whole tendency is to move in the opposite direction, far to the right of Brecht. He seems always to be trying to tug the film back to the social reality the play sprang from. . . ."[11] The last remark is accurate, but it is far from correct to see Pabst's aesthetic compromise as a political gesture to the right of Brecht since Pabst's film succeeds in communicating the social message of the piece more artfully than Brecht would admit, even though it lacks the didacticism of his original scheme. A film record of Brecht's production might have proved enlightening, but it is doubtful that it would be as engaging as Pabst's film version.

Whether or not one takes issue with Brecht or Pabst, it is undeniable that in the German version Pabst is in superb command of a memorable cast. Rudolf Forster's suave, cool incarnation of Mackie Messer blends perfectly the sharpness of Brecht's character with a roguishness and poised romanticism with striking effect. In the

French version, Albert Préjean is less impressive, investing the role with a light, airy incongruous Gallic charm. As Freddy Buache has observed, Forster keeps his hands in his pockets while kissing Polly, while Préjean throws his arms about her with an effusive romatic air.

Carola Neher, who was executed by the Nazis in 1940, effectively recreates her stage role as Polly, as does the irreplaceable Lotte Lenya as Jenny, both demonstrating the staccato-like method of singing that Brecht preferred. Florelle, who the *cinéphile* will remember as the young bride in Jean Vigo's *L'Atalante*, is Polly in the French version, and though she is prettier than Neher, she is less vigorous; but the excellent *chanteuse*, Margo Lion, who had previously studied in Germany, is as equally memorable a Jenny as the famous Lenya, displaying many of the same vocal traits.

Gaston Modot's Peachum is less antipathetic than Fritz Rasp in the German version, giving the character a more humanistic dimension, while Jack Henley's "Tiger" Brown in the French version fails entirely to convey the blustering, comic qualities that make Reinhold Schunzel's interpretation so memorable. On the other hand, Antonin Artaud, in the small role of the beggar who transforms himself with accessories furnished by Peachum and laughs at his reflection in a mirror, is incomparable in the otherwise mellow Gallicized version.

Dreigroschenoper found Pabst at the peak of his creative powers; and although it is one of his most popular films, owning to its recent re-release, it is important because it reveals the strengths of his art, thematically and pictorially. The plot's sociopolitical import was clearly in line with his thinking; and the theme of love and friendship, which is so important in his next film, is implied as a solace for the unscrupulous and desperate characters. With the aid of a fine cast of actors, designers, musicians, a brilliant cameraman, and a trio of skilled screenwriters, Pabst provides us with a well-balanced orchestration blending Brecht's dry, pithy, social critique into an elegant world of light and shadow all his own.

Kameradschaft: *European Solidarity*

In 1958, at the Exposition Universelle de Bruxelles, *Kameradschaft*, the concluding film in Pabst's social trilogy, ranked twenty-six in a poll of critics who selected the thirty most important films in the history of cinema. It is still held in high esteem, and rightly so, because it is one of the cinema's most beautiful and durable achievements. In *Westfront* Pabst expressed his hatred of a war that destroyed the very social institutions it was waged to defend. In *Kameradschaft* he speaks openly, not as a brilliant creator of atmosphere or the interpreter of a musical satire or novel, but as *auteur* and humanist, advocating a position of fraternalism in which he believed.

Although German culture and art unquestionably provided the ground of inspiration for Pabst's art, he increasingly became opposed to the intense patriotic nationalism of his countrymen. Following *Dreigroschenoper,* he had planned to film the life of Toussaint L'Ouverture, the black general who organized a slave rebellion in Haiti and who was finally arrested by Napoleon and died in a French fortress. Like so many other cherished projects of Pabst, it came to nothing for lack of financial support. But its subject indicates a general tendency, a conviction that in order for civilization to survive, men must struggle to transcend national, political, and ethnic differences. This ethical precept now took the form of comradeship of workers in a time of crisis, a strength that could unite divergent political sectors into one vast European community. It is easy, in retrospect, to find this position, couched in the rhetoric of Marxist idealism, blindly optimistic at a time when Germany was already on the brink of a political crisis; but it in no way diminishes the power of its appeal, executed with great imaginative skill.

The idea for *Kameradschaft* originated in a newspaper account of a mining disaster that occurred at Courrières in 1906, where more than twelve hundred men died. Pabst locates the situation, however, at Lorraine in 1919 at a mine on the Franco-German border, separated into respective sections by the official frontier. Thus, time and setting are sharply tuned to a recent confrontation of nationalist feelings. The scenario was drawn up by Pabst's faithful associate, Ladislaus Vajda, with the assistance of Karl Otten and Peter Martin Lampel, from a story outline by Otten.

Organized as a co-production, the production was financed by Nero Films in Berlin and Franco-Film-Aubert in Paris, with general supervision again under Seymour Nebenzahl. The settings for the mine galleries were carefully constructed by engineers and designers under the supervision of Ernö Metzner and Karl Vollbrecht on the Staaken studio stages near Berlin at enormous expense. Not only did this allow for a scrupulous naturalism but freed the camera to move about at will and in conjunction with precise lighting effects. Miniatures are used only briefly in the flooding sequences.

The remainder of the film was shot entirely on location in mining towns in Lens, Bethune, and Gelsenkirchen on both sides of the border.

In selecting his cast, Pabst chose German and French actors and had them speak their respective languages, a natural barrier that bears pointed significance in the screenplay. Ernst Bush, who appeared as the Strassensänger in *Dreigroschenoper*, portrays Wittkopp, leader of the German miners, supported by well-known German players, Fritz Kampers, Gustav Puttjer, and Alexander Granach. The French cast, headed by Georges Charlia, Daniel Mandaille, and Andrée Ducret, is less familiar, but significantly provides much of the film's emotional appeal, suggesting Pabst's feeling that the intermingling of French sentiment into Germanic culture had a humanizing influence.

A symbolic prelude, situated near the surface border between the mining camps, establishes the seeds of conflict. Two small boys, one French, the other German, engage in a lively game of marbles. The camera pans to a nearby road following some German miners headed for the frontier to apply for work; they are turned back by the French, and as they pass by, a dispute erupts between the boys in the foreground. Pabst then cuts directly to the German sector of the mine tunnel where a miner expresses concern over a fire that has started on the French side of the mine. In the French galleries, the camera tracks stealthily into the recesses of the shaft to reveal the smoldering menace, while orders are issued to repair a weakened wall to curtail its pathway.

A nocturnal excursion of three Germans into a French beer hall places the conflict on a personal level. Led by Wilderer, a blustering but sincere worker, the trio manage to communicate their order to the bartender. On the dance floor Wilderer is attracted to Françoise who is with her fiancé, Jean, a French miner. Summoning up his courage with proper French phrases, Wilderer approaches her for a dance; her curt refusal, however, leaves no doubt as to her feelings about Germans. When she learns of the fire in the mine, she threatens to leave Jean if he persists in exposing himself to the danger. Not only is the beer hall, with its smoky, fluid ambience a Pabstian milieu par excellence, but it serves as a significant field of social interaction, and the moving camera captures the various paths of departure as the people stroll through the dark streets of the little mining town.

The domestic atmosphere of Jean's home—probably a set rather than an actual location—is captured in realistic detail the following morning as Françoise, perturbed by Jean's insistence on returning to the mines to help in the rescue operations, prepares to leave the household. Paralleling underground events with those on the surface, Pabst moves to the mine where a thundering explosion sucks the dreaded fire down the corridors, then to Françoise attempting to disembark from a moving train after the alarm at the mine shaft signals a disaster. As news quickly spreads through the little town, the camera captures candid responses of the anxious populace, and the rapid cutting reminds us of the early experiments of Eisenstein (*Strike*) and Pudovkin (*Mother*) with their turbulent imagery of the proletarian masses.

By contrasting the subsequent events in the mine with the attendant turmoil and anguish of the crowds on the surface, Pabst establishes a formal structural dialectic that continues throughout the entire film. Guards are ordered to hold fast a grilled iron gateway against a torrent of wives and relatives struggling to gain access to the area near the mine entrance, with low camera angles accentuating the tension and agitated movement. An elderly man, intent on retrieving his grandson, Georges, eludes the guards and descends the mine shaft by a maze of stairways and ladders. As Françoise joins the agitated mob at the gate, a section of the mine caves in, leaving the remaining miners trapped.

In the distant German camp the miners ending the night shift gather in a massive shower room. This intimate glimpse into the daily lives of workers is transformed into a panorama of glistening movements; long ropes carry grime-ridden uniforms into the rafters of the building, and masses of nude male flesh in the showers reflect light from wet surfaces.

Wittkopp finally airs the question on all their minds. "Have they rescue equipment?" "Who cares?" answers one of his comrades, "they are richer than we." But Wittkopp is not dissuaded, reminding them of the wives and children awaiting news of the fate of the Frenchmen trapped below, and with a tone of authority, he asserts "We *must* help!" arousing the collective consent of those around him. At the director's office, they request permission to take a truck and rescue apparatus to the aid of the French. Pabst's editor, Jean Oser, recalls that a scene had been written in which the workers meet resistance from the owners, but brush them aside to take

matters into their own hands. However, because the workers in the
camp in which Pabst was shooting disapproved of the scene, it was
not filmed. The alternate scene, however, has a similar effect, as the
director, his authority indicated by his position *above* the workers
on a stairway, reluctantly agrees to their proposal, then immediately
phones the French officials, muttering, "Well, I'll take the credit."

Efforts of the French rescue team are meanwhile filmed with a
detailed, documentary precision, while a subjective camera
explores the rubble and corpses below, with smoke and *clair-obscur*
lighting imparting authenticity along with a halo of imaginative terror. A wall collapses and several galleries are flooded. The tempo
becomes faster as several points of action are intercut with exciting
effect: the old man's desperate search for his grandson among the
dead, the return of the injured to the surface, the seething crowd of
women pressing against the iron gate, and the advance of the German rescue party.

The French crowd is astounded at the arrival of the German
miners. "Les Allemagnes! Ce n'est pas possible!" exclaims Françoise. Meanwhile, the old man revives his grandson below while the
Germans join the French rescuers in their mine, their union stated
with an emphatic close-up of hands clasping, recalling the final
fraternal image of *Westfront*. Wilderer and his companion in the
German sector decide to join them and do not hesitate to demolish
the symbolic iron trellis marking the 1919 frontier to gain entrance
to the French galleries.

While the quieted crowds keep vigil by night as the dead are
recovered and the injured given medical treatment, in the depths
below Wilderer and his friend discover the grandfather and boy in a
stable room. Language problems and a forced *bonhomie* are poignant without falling into cliché. The flooding of the room forces
them to another chamber where their escape path is subsequently
blocked, while the rescue party, now bearing gas masks, locates
survivors by tapping code on a network of pipes.

Pabst's pervasive realism is heightened by a symbolic sequence
that is admirable for its psychological impact and its modern conception of subjective flashback. A French miner, almost overcome by
gas fumes, is discovered by a German whose face is transformed by
a gas mask. Hearing the man address him in German, the Frenchman experiences a hallucinatory relapse and, imagining himself
back in the war attacks his rescuer. The intercutting of brief shots of

battle—recalling the landscapes of *Westfront*—give a startlingly surreal note to the dramatic confrontation.

Contrasting with this flare of intense emotion, an engaging humor and tension derive from the attempts of trapped Germans to locate a ringing telephone, and with the resolution of their efforts, and a note of elation in their limited French, the party is assured of imminent rescue.

The final sequence ties together character relationships severed by the film's main action: the reconciliation of the lovers, of Françoise and her brother, and the general reunion of the survivors of the tragedy with their families. The locale is identical to that of the prelude: the surface demarcation of the mine's division into sectors. Here, for once, Pabst allows the theme to be expressed in verbal terms, spelling out its social and political implications. The German representative recalls the Treaty of Versailles and the undeniably bitter feelings that arose as a result between Germany and France. Yet, he claims, bonds of human sympathy and obligation always remain steadfast in the hearts of the workers, sharing common problems in a brotherhood that does not acknowledge military or government alignments.

The French spokesman responds with an eloquent and similarly moving speech that is met with enthusiastic applause. "It is because we are *all* miners that you have saved us. . . . We have only two common enemies—*Gas* and *War!*" This spirited oratory, summing up the theme already expressed more subtly in narrative terms, tends to weaken its effect artistically, and is comparable to the frequent propaganda speeches that occur in early Soviet sound films, like Dovzhenko's *Schors.*

The epilogue, which casts a rather ironic shadow on the film's thesis, has one French and one German official, separated by new iron trellis at the underground frontier, ratifying its reestablishment. The grim humor recalls some of the dry disenchantment of *Dreigroschenoper,* subtly suggesting what Kracauer calls a "victory of bureaucratic wisdom." It was conveniently eliminated by German censors and is missing from the American release prints in circulation today. The French version, with only slight differences and retitled *La Tragédie de la mine,* retains the scene, however, as well as a brief exchange between Jean and Françoise that is missing from the German prints.

The reactionary Hugenberg press in Germany found *Kamerad-*

schaft shockingly unpatriotic while generally acknowledging the artistic qualities it demonstrated, following its Berlin premiere on November 17, 1931. At the time, Germany was experiencing severe problems as a result of unemployment and any film that advocated proletarian unification was correctly identified as radical. Indeed, Pabst's was one of the few films of the 1930s to examine the daily lives, attitudes, and feelings of the European working class in their natural environment. Its only near rival was Slatan Dudow's *Kuhle Wampe* (released in the U.S. as *Whither Germany?*), made in 1932 from an original screenplay by Bertolt Brecht. Its strong pro-Communist, pro-labor views quickly met with opposition and led to virtual bankruptcy over lawsuits.

Kracauer's evaluation, while mirroring a certain admiration, refuses to consider the film in any other than abstract, conceptual terms: "Pabst's film marks a progress in theoretical thought; for he now tries to make his pacifism invulnerable by endorsing the socialist doctrine. . . . [He] advocates the international solidarity of workers, characterizing them as pioneers of a society in which national egoism, the eternal source of wars, will be abolished."[12]

Aside from the explicit rhetoric of the final sequence, Pabst's doctrine—if it can be categorized as such—is founded in terms of dramatized reality rather than in theory. It is for this reason that *Kameradschaft* is frequently cited as a masterful example of the fictional documentary, influencing British poetic realists like Basil Wright, Humphrey Jennings, and Alberto Cavalcanti. Certainly, not only the mine galleries, but a supporting cast of unpolished nonprofessionals, are as authentic in appearance as their surroundings. But *Kameradschaft* is also a formal triumph. Brilliant contrasts of fire, water, and smoke are constantly utilized expressively by cinematographer Fritz Arno Wagner, complementing the detailed semblance of daily life in the mining camps. As in *Westfront*, sound is pared down to minimal effect, with no background score, insistence on dual languages, and careful attention to natural but evocative effects, particularly the rhythmic tapping on piping in the mine.

Kameradschaft is the work of an artist ultimately more involved with people and human feelings than with ideas or class struggle, marking the limitation and strength of his art. The French must have understood this and appreciated it for they immediately acclaimed the film a masterpiece, and shortly after its premiere in

Paris, Pabst was awarded the coveted Legion of Honor by the French government for furthering the cause of friendship between people and countries.

5

The French Period

Timeless Morality and Myth:
L'Atlantide (Die Herrin von Atlantis)

THE ENTHUSIASTIC REPUTATION that Pabst enjoyed in France as a result of *Dreigroschenoper* and *Kameradschaft* prompted producer Seymour Nebenzahl of Nero Films to engage him for a three-language production. Pabst showed an interest in Pierre Benoit's novel, *L'Atlantide*, which had been superbly mounted on an extravagant scale by the French director Jacques Feyder as a silent film in 1921. Pabst's new German, English, and French versions, shot in three months and on a comparatively modest budget, proved equally successful, artistically and commercially. Because the subject lacked an obviously controversial theme, critics in Germany praised Pabst's achievement and belatedly hailed him as a great director.

L'Atlantide is an exotic French adventure set in the deserts of North Africa. Pabst's treatment of it is cool and Germanic, without sacrificing the sensuous aspects that become more emphatic in the French version. The scenario—combining the efforts of Alexandre Arnoux, Jacques Duval, and Ladislaus Vajda—follows the surface action of Benoit's novel closely, but emphasis is shifted from the exotic and spectacular to a controlled ritualistic atmosphere, bringing into relief certain social motifs and psychological tropes that are peculiarly Pabstian. In place of the elaborate Art Nouveau settings and costumes of Feyder's silent version, Pabst utilizes an austere simplicity of visual contrasts and achieves a more modern psychological effect with the chiselled features of Brigitte Helm in the role of Antinéa as opposed to the pulchritudinous posturings and vampirism of Stacia Napierkowska.

The film opens with a radio announcer relating the history of the lost, mythical city of Atlantis as Pabst cuts to a shot of Saint-Avit listening to the broadcast at a desert outpost in the Sahara, where he begins to recall the past two years to his friend, Lieutenant Ferrières. These events, seen in flashback, constitute the major dramatic construction.

The account of the lost desert patrol is relatively disappointing, full of contrived melodramatic touches and dreadful dialogue reminiscent of the pulp serial; the discovery of an awakening "corpse" leads to some pretentious philosophizing about death and life. A nocturnal attack by desert tribesmen, for all its visual vigor, suffers from primitive sound recording. But Pabst finds his medium in staging the bizarre, surreal experience of Saint-Avit. Searching in desperation for his companion, Captain Morhange, he wanders dazed through the streets of a strange city, unnoticed, accompanied by the disquieting chant of native singers. The incongruous sight of tribesmen listening to a Rossini overture on a Victrola in an open square among deserted, glistening white wall surfaces, creates an abstract, dreamlike dislocation, sustained by the slow, rhythmic pacing of his abductors as they carry him into the depths of the underground city.

Awakening in the shadowy, labyrinthine world of Atlantis, Saint-Avit is intrigued by reflections in a pool that seem to mirror a magical landscape out of Cocteau's *Orphée*. He is welcomed by a charming and eccentric Count Bielowsky and is fascinated by a drunken and depressed Norwegian, driven to despair by the wiles of Antinéa, whose desire is the command of all those who surround her.

Saint-Avit's initial encounter with the love goddess is a mysterious, virtually wordless ritual, climaxed by a particularly memorable chess game through which Pabst registers the encroaching snare of hypnotic sexual passion to which the lieutenant almost succumbs. Recovering from the spell, he demands his liberty and repeatedly inquires after his friend, Morhange. Still, his face registers the intoxication of Antinéa's beauty, commemorated in a monumental sculpture of her classic face that later becomes a sacrificial altar. Celebrating Antinéa's new conquest, the garrulous count discloses her origins in a quintessentially Pabstian scene that owes nothing to Benoit's tale. "Antinéa, c'est Paris," reveals the count, and suddenly we are transported to a line of can-can dancers in a bistro which introduces Clémentine, a dancer, that he matches with a desert chieftain; but, unexpectedly, we learn that the count himself fathered the dancer's child.

Meanwhile, Antinéa is frightened by a sorceress's forecast of an imminent death. Before her mirror, reflecting an image of consuming passion and narcissism, she vows that *she* will not die. To reveal Antinéa's covert liaison with Morhange, Pabst uses especially brilliant staging that captures virtually the entire sequence of shifting psychological centers in one sustained camera movement. Saint-Avit chances upon Antinéa's attempt to seduce Morhange, whom she actually loves. Stung by his rejection, she angrily dismisses him, while the camera tracks from Saint-Avit's hiding place to disclose another eavesdropper, Tanit-Zerga, a servant who secretly loves Saint-Avit. Inflamed by his discovery, Saint-Avit denounces Antinéa, but a wave of jealousy induces him to carry out her order to kill Morhange. (In the silent version, a drugged cigarette provides the motivation.) Pabst adds a personal note in showing Saint-Avit's friendship overcoming impulsive sexual desire, albeit too late, as he embraces the dying Morhange, then is restrained from a murderous attack on the triumphant Antinéa before her sphinx-like shrine.

Saint-Avit's escape, effected with the aid of the faithful Tanit-Zerga, is similar to Feyder's version, with the added note of conscience-stricken grief over the death of Morhange. In the tragic and desolate scenes of the girl's death in the desert and the lieutenant's desperate struggle for survival, the relentless tracking camera sustains a rhythm and poetic intensity that Feyder's tableaux effects cannot equal. Instead of having Saint-Avit simply return to Antinéa while thought to be suffering from hallucinations, Pabst concludes with a dramatic sandstorm that drives back the search party, headed by Ferrières.

As in *Kameradschaft*, two distinctly contrasted visual fields are created by a sensuous interaction of light and décor. Ernö Metzner's endless maze of cavelike corridors, stairways, and columns in the subterranean Atlantis are given a spacial articulation by sinuous camera movements, recalling many similar moments in his *Kameradschaft* mine galleries and the flickering underworld ambience of *Die Dreigroschenoper*. Contrasted with this artificial environment are the shimmering expanses of sand—actual locations near Hoggar in the Sahara—and the luminous reflected light of the desert town. For the first time, Pabst had the good fortune to have at his disposal the sensitive camera of Eugen Schüfftan, who was to

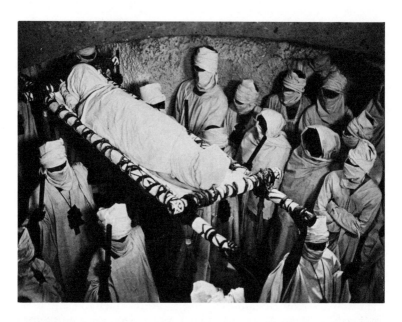

Two scenes: Catafalque and camels from L'Atlantide

photograph three of his subsequent French films. Adding impetus to the imagery is a fine music score by Wolfgang Zeller, fusing native African rhythms with romantic and modern styles in a cohesive and satisfying manner.

With his study of the mythical siren of Atlantis, Pabst once again takes up his study of feminine psychological obsessions. Brigitte Helm, whom he had used previously in *Abwege,* and *Jeanne Ney* projects an intense, smoldering beauty more akin to the statuesque presence of Dietrich or Garbo than the innocent sensuality of Louise Brooks. Pabst uses her as a sensual object, as a magnetic field of attraction in his study of a classic *femme fatale* whose every glance and movement is a reflection of a destructive, consuming sexual power. Pierre Blanchar is more sensitive as Saint-Avit in the French version than Heinz Klingenberg as his German counterpart; but Gustav Diessl's Morhange in the German version *(Die Herrin von Atlantis)* is younger and more convincing than Jean Angelo, who recreated his role in the Feyder version for Pabst.

Vladimir Sokoloff as the Hetman of Jitomir or Count Bielowsky (whose counterpart in the silent version is a senile librarian) is the most Pabstian of the characters, worldly, cunning, and affectionate, richly evocative of a decadent European sophistication. His flashback introduces in microcosm the Pabstian milieu par excellence, with reference to the Europeanization inferred by the radio announcer ("No European has reached or has been known to return. . .") and by the interpolation of the phonograph and Parisian cocktails. Antinéa and her retinue are symbolic of a spiritually decaying society, struggling between the confines of dream and reality to maintain its traditions, but withdrawing further and further into an inaccessible legend incarnated in the figure of Antinéa herself. In what is superficially nothing more than a tale of adventure and romantic intrigue, a covert vision emerges. As Yves Aubry and Jacques Pétat see it: "Pabst knew how to render visually perceptible the mechanism that leads to the death of the last representatives of that society, whose agony he never ceased to portray."[1]

Don Quichotte

Miguel de Cervantes' famous picaresque novel *Don Quixote* has always proved a source of inspiration for film makers. Silent versions were made in France (1909), America (1916), Britain (1923), and Denmark (1926). Pabst's was the first of the sound versions, and it

remains the most curious, idiosyncratic, and ultimately unsatisfying, especially when compared to Grigori Kozintsev's memorable
realization from 1957, with the great Russian actor, Nicolai Cher-
kassov.

Pabst's editor, Jean Oser, in his *Cinemages* interview relates the
ill-fated conditions under which the production was conceived and
executed. The idea of filming a multilingual version of *Don Quixote*
originated with a Greek financier in London who wanted Chaplin to
direct and Maurice Ravel to compose a special score. The project
was poorly organized and was on the verge of floundering when
Pabst, who had journeyed to France on a business transaction, was
asked to direct on the basis of his recent success with *L'Atlantide*.
Drawn to the prospect of filming Cervantes, he agreed and brought
on his own scenarist, Alexandre Arnoux, set designer Andrei Andreiev, as well as Jean Oser, though he was unable to influence the
casting. More unfortunate, however, was the fact that he was unable
to complete the film planned. After about seventy percent of the
shooting was done, the budget was depleted, and in order to salvage
the film Pabst was forced to pad the length to about ninety minutes
with some additional songs composed by Jacques Ibert.

The consortium of producers—Vandor, Nelson, and Webster,—
had obviously conceived the project as a vehicle for the Russian
basso Fyodor Chaliapin, whose physical being and operatic lyricism
are the dominant focal points. Parker Tyler observes that "like Don
Quixote, like Cervantes himself, Chaliapin was an old man, an old
man in whom a magnificently expressive voice survived in the way
the ideal of chivalry had survived in Don Quixote de la Mancha."[2]
The adaptation by Paul Morand and Alexandre Arnoux reduced the
rambling structure of the novel to a few key episodes that draw on
the essential comic nobility of the Don's misplaced idealism and
give Pabst an opportunity to expand on the theme of social hypocrisy.

A prologue opens on the Cervantes manuscript, springing magi-
cally to life in a brief comic sequence conceived by animator Lotte
Reiniger in Chinese shadows, accompanied by Ibert's jaunty score.
In a musty corner of his library, the Don extols the virtues of
knighthood and daydreams of a beautiful Dulcinea. The only solace
of age is found in his wonderful books, the acquisition of which has
impoverished him and left his household in disorder. His subjective
musing and fantasy are given over to the stylized dimension of song.

Fédor Chaliapin in the title role of Don Quichotte

The Don's precious madness is given new logic when he interrupts a theatrical performance that belittles the cause of virtue. Inspired by the stories of old, he is deemed Knight of the Mournful Countenance by Merlin the Magician, and subsequently embarks on his faithful steed Rosinante to combat the injustice and evil of the world. Joined by Sancho, a philandering, sniveling, hen-pecked servant, he roams the countryside, protected by a shield and coat of armor.

Pabst's conception of the Spanish landscape is stark and unadorned, but, in sharply contrasting interiors, lighting produces some of the langorous atmosphere of Impressionism. Shooting on locations in Southern France, Pabst makes use of brilliant sunlight and natural objects in an unromanticized context. Sheep on a country road are denounced by the Don as obstacles to his freedom, and his liberation of chained convicts only provokes them to stone him. Stopping in a village, the Don imagines he has found his Dulcinea in a common milkmaid and rejoices when Sancho acquires a steel cap to replace his lost helmet.

As the knightly mission becomes more urgent, Pabst interweaves the unrest at the Don's home resulting from his inexplicable departure. Hypocrisy and superstition rear their heads as his daughter becomes engaged to Carasco, an insipid, doleful youth eager for a dowry; Sancho's shrewish wife begins to bemoan her spouse's fate; and the local priest interprets the Don's mysterious madness as a sign of divine retribution.

Cornered by a party of soldiers at an inn, the Don and Sancho are amazed at being at last rewarded for their efforts. Amid the elegant world of courtiers and Spanish aristocracy they are honored guests of a duke and duchess who have been made aware of their exploits and plot to cure them once and for all of their folly by matching the Don in a tournament against Carasco, his daughter's fiancé. The Don touchingly dedicates his performance to the eternal beauty of Dulcinea while the duchess murmurs ironically, "only madmen truly know how to love." But Sancho, tossed in the air on a blanket, is made to look the fool, while the Don, proving himself against his maladroit opponent, is severely offended at discovering the plot to dishonor him.

Departing the court and driven by wounded pride and all-consuming passion, he fearlessly attacks a windmill—ignoring Sancho's vain protest—which he imagines to be a giant. Knocked from his horse and made to look ridiculous by the inexorable movement of the mill, he is beaten by a reality against which all his rebellion is powerless. Weakened by the defeat, he is removed to his home in a wooden cage, like some mysterious and rare species of animal. In the town square he witnesses the burning of his library, blamed for his "corruption," and finally dies in the arms of his beloved Sancho and his daughter.

Don Quichotte is ultimately unsatisfying, for all its brilliant moments, because it is incomplete. The scenes of court life and Carasco's plot to marry the Don's daughter are too brief to suggest the character development intended. Nevertheless, even within its limitations, Pabst's articulation of visual space by composition and editing are often admirable, particularly the emphasis on low camera angles on Chaliapin that point up his *hauteur*. In the moving, lyrical conclusion, Pabst brings to bear his eloquent visual powers. The contrast of fire and nocturnal shadow, filmed with fine chiaroscuro effect, illuminates the remote, sympathetic faces of the crowd gathering around the dying Don as they watch his books burn, a symbolic punishment for transgression dictated by the priest.

As the camera slowly moves from the dying figure, through the crowd of mute observers, to the sorrowful Sancho embracing his donkey, the screen radiates a passage of strong pathos. Not only does Pabst evoke the flames of the Inquisition, but more immediately conflagrations prepetrated by the Nazis against works by dissident writers. While the camera lingers on the flames, consuming the Don's knowledge and dreams, his dirge is sounded by Chaliapin. Then, with a final poetic touch, Pabst returns to the dimension of myth by reversing the destructive force of the fire, reconstituting the title page with which he begins: "Don Quixote de la Mancha by Miguel de Cervantes."

Parker Tyler, who rates the film highly, finds that the differences between it and the novel are not important. "Pabst's work is a creative interpretation rightly based mainly on the all-powerful apparition of a strong Don, not a silly one; a frustrated 'Samson' of romanticism, not a posturing relic."[3] Chaliapin's authoritative performance still remains persuasive as an aristocratic dreamer, but Dorville's comic Sancho Panza, whose earthy common sense and realism counter the Don's idealism, proves, like George Robey in the English version, too vulgar and sentimental and fails to win our sympathy as he should.

More significant, however, is the fact that in the context of Pabst's career *Don Quichotte* can now be seen as a poignant reflection of the director's own ultimate defeat, a chronicle of his own idealism as opposed to his actual achievement. Thus, in 1954, Italian critics Lina del Fra and Tito Guerrini insinuate that "*Don Quichotte* is not only the filmmaker's autobiography, it is his spiritual testament."[4] The windmills of war, nationalism, and social injustice could no longer be combatted by artistic means, and the years ahead were destined to be laden with disappointment, frustration, and unrealized projects.

While Pabst was putting the final touches on *Don Quichotte*, Hitler was made Chancellor in the January elections of 1933, causing the celebrated director to remain in France where he was to find refuge for six years.

Exotic Melodrama and "Poetic" Realism

The dislocation of Pabst's career from Germany to France seems to have been a personally, if not artistically, rewarding move that he hoped would offer a climate of growth. In a 1933 interview with French critic Louis Gerbe, his optimism and spirits were high:

"While in Germany, I was reproached for my humanist and pacifist tendencies and for having introduced politics into my films, I was welcomed to France with signs of esteem, even on the part of my adversaries. Thus, M. Bailby, when he was still director of *Intran* at the time of his residence in Nice, told me that while he did not at all share my social opinions, he was full of admiration for the manner in which I expressed them in my films. Further, in France, the culture in general is very affable. The middle class, guardians of the best intellectual traditions, virtually disappearing in Germany, is fortunately still intact in the country of Voltaire, Rousseau, and Diderot. . ."[5]

The intellectual and cultural milieu of which Pabst speaks failed, however, to stimulate any subsequent important work. In spite of the fact that some themes can be linked to earlier preoccupations, the films of the French period sustain the level of routine melodrama, often beautifully photographed, due to the camera of Eugen Schüfftan, and the use of much first-rate French acting talent. But, as Henri Langlois states it, "the years spent in France are for the art of Pabst, lost years. His eye was always both penetrating and fleeting, but he no longer expressed himself. I think Pabst is an illustration of that rule that says certain plants cannot grow as soon as they are transplanted elsewhere."[6] Although the films do bear out Langlois's judgment, their relative obscurity and occasional memorable moments make them worthy of brief mention.

In 1933, following the successful launching of *Don Quichotte*, Pabst wanted to do a film about a famous lawyer who defied prejudice by defending Jews in Hungary, but was unable to find financial backing. At the suggestion of Tobis Films he agreed to direct a "slice of life" story based on a play by Ladislaus Bus-Fekete. *Du Haut en Bas* was a French attempt at comedy of manners, concerning various people who live in a boarding house in an old section of Vienna and their lives, loves, and foibles. There is Bodeletz, a ruined gambler who persists in testing his martingales with dried beans; Madame Binder, a fat lady who lives below him and ultimately succeeds in winning his love; a former dressmaker who luxuriates in the discovery of the wireless; and the idol of the quarter, Charles Boulla, a young football player, who is disappointed in love.

Although Pabst and his set designer, Ernö Metzner, were both intimately familiar with Vienna and its inhabitants, and constructed a flexible and detailed background for the action, the predominantly

French cast and dialogue fail to establish anything of a Viennese character. One can imagine Max Ophüls or Jean Renoir handling the subject with great dexterity and warmth, but Pabst's direction remains oddly detached and craftsmanlike. Thus, *Du Haut en Bas* disappointed critics and audiences alike, though it is still pleasurable to observe Michel Simon's sensitive interpretation of the gambler, the film début of Jean Gabin as the young athlete, and Peter Lorre in a brief appearance as a beggar.

Hollywood Excursion: *A Modern Hero*

The failure of *Du Haut en Bas* left Pabst in a precarious position. In France money was difficult to obtain for film production and producers were interested only in profitable projects. Warner Brothers, who had partially financed *Die Dreigroschenoper,* had earlier invited Pabst to direct a film in Hollywood; but as he knew little of production methods in America, he was reluctant to accept. Now, however, he relented, feeling that he had little to lose under the circumstances.

Unlike Murnau, who arrived at Fox Studios with a finished script for *Sunrise* in hand, Pabst had nothing to present Warners and for months he looked at various proposals made by the studio, none of which interested him. Finally, he settled on *A Modern Hero,* from a novel by the popular writer Louis Bromfield, adapted for the screen by Katherine Scola and Gene Markey.

Set in the Midwest, the story focuses on Pierre, an ambitious young circus performer, who gives up his circus career and his love for a small-town girl—who later bears his child—for a wealthy widow who loans him funds to establish a bicycle business with an inventive genius. Using women as social stepping-stones, Pierre becomes a wealthy automobile manufacturer and secretly supports his illegitimate son, but ultimately loses his fortune in a stock swindle and his son in an accident. Penniless and broken in spirit, he returns to his mother, the girl he left behind, and the circus, where he finds courage to face the future.

Pabst's ignorance of life in the Midwest and his lack of interest in the basic material were initial handicaps. He managed to give the circus scenes some visual exuberance, but saddled with a dialogue director, Arthur Grenville Collins, who allowed the cast to overact any attempts at subtlety disappeared. Richard Barthelmess, a former matinee idol, who had starred in Henry King's memorable

Tol'able David in 1921, was far from credible as the youthful Pierre. Whatever psychological motivation and atmosphere Pabst had managed to squeeze from this tale of a young capitalist's rise and fall was duly eliminated when his work was cut down by the studio to a thin, quick seventy minutes, conforming to the fast-paced Warner Brothers style of the 1930s.

Pabst had to agree with the reviewers that *A Modern Hero* was a flop, and later asked that it not be included in his filmography. Meanwhile, at Paramount Pictures he worked for months developing a screenplay from an original idea in which he took great interest. *War is Declared*, which was to have starred Peter Lorre, revived themes that were close to Pabst. The story concerned a radio operator aboard a large transatlantic liner who becomes mentally unstable and repeats communications from his wartime experience, announcing that war has been declared and thousands have been killed in bombed cities. The tranquil, friendly atmosphere of the ship becomes divided into combative camps along nationalist lines. When they ultimately learn of the hoax, they are shocked into a realization of their folly and are made to realize their common humanity. *War is Declared*, if made, could possibly have established Pabst in America and given an entirely different direction to his life and career. However, when word reached Washington of the story's political implications, Paramount was induced to drop their plans to film it.

Pabst was bitterly disillusioned by the repressive system of Hollywood's assembly-line methods where he had virtually no creative control and was regarded primarily as a functionary rather than an artist. His sentiments were made clear in an essay, "Servitude et grandeur à Hollywood," published in 1937 after his return to France:

> . . . If in Europe for a number of years (at the moment, here, it is becoming extremely difficult) the director was able to put his mark on a film, in Hollywood this was always impossible: there the director has neither artistic nor financial responsibility; he is only one of numerous links in a chain formed of diverse departments through which films are manufactured. . . . The director received the subject of the film in the form of a shot breakdown with close details. He cannot change a word or modify a camera angle without authorization. . . .[7]

Unlike his compatriot, Fritz Lang, who was to arrive in Hollywood in 1935, Pabst lacked the arrogant, hard-nosed tenacity and ruthlessness to survive in the Hollywood studio. Whereas Lang pursued a demonic, nightmare vision in terms of American crime drama and forced the studios to accept him, Pabst was too sensitive and open to the suggestions of others. He needed people like Marc Sorkin, Ladislaus Vajda, Leo Lania, Andreiev, and Seymour Nebenzahl to work with; and if France had proved accommodating, the cactus-garden environment of California was decidedly not.

The following year (1935) Pabst left for New York to plan a film version of Gounod's opera *Faust,* to star Lawrence Tibbett, but at the last minute, financing was withdrawn and the frustrated, embattled director departed for another period of exile in France.

France and New Frustrations

Back in Paris, producer Romain Pinès persuaded Pabst that a combination of psychological realism with exotic locations would stimulate the director's visual gifts in *Mademoiselle Docteur,* also known as *Salonique, nid d'espions.* The story is roughly based on the real life of German spy Anne Marie Lesser, who died during World War II and whose life had already been the basis of an MGM film, *Stamboul Quest,* in 1934.

Pabst's film begins in Paris during World War I, shifts to Berlin, thence to Bern, and concludes in Salonica, where "Mademoiselle Docteur" is sent to reestablish communication between Berlin and German spies in Greece. Posing as an American journalist, she falls in love with Captain Carrère (Pierre Fresnay). To effect her capture, the French employ Condoyan (Pierre Blanchar), a Greek double agent who is also working for Germany. In an attempt to steal important documents, she is exposed by Gaby, the Greek's girl friend. Finally, declared insane, she is put in an asylum. In spite of the obvious contrivances of the scenario, Pabst manages to evoke sincere performances from his cast and with his expert cinematographer creates an appropriate atmosphere in the variegated locales of the story.

French historian, Freddy Buache, writes of the film with obvious affection: "A décor, a costume, an attitude of an actor and the intensity of light create the atmosphere in establishing the drama. One does not forget the impression given by Jouvet as a vegetable merchant who continually chews on a straw, nor the prying and alarming looks of a disquieting Blanchar. . . . As for Fresnay, he seems to repeat his role in *La Grande Illusion.* And Barrault lights up when they cut a slice of melon for him."[8] In addition, Buache praises its visualization, as well as acting skill. "Schüfftan treats space with a superlative mastery of lighting. He animates the acting areas which Pabst, through his direction of the actors and his montage, puts to good use. Some sections could be ranked among the most successful plastic efforts of the French cinema before the war."[9]

The commercial success of *Mademoiselle Docteur* encouraged Romain Pinès to secure Pabst once again for *Le Drame de Shanghai* in 1938. The exotic, melodramatic plot revolves around Kay, a Russian cabaret singer, played by Christiane Mardayne, who serves as a tool of the Japanese "Black Dragon" terrorist society and tries to break away from the spy ring when her daughter returns from school in Hong Kong. Threatened by Ivan, another member of the ring, Kay kills him and sacrifices her own life so that her daughter can escape with the aid of a journalist when the Chinese revolt against the Japanese terrorists.

According to Herman Weinberg and Leopold Boehm, Pabst saw the story as an expression of social protest in which he allied himself with the Chinese progressivists in their efforts to expel the Japanese terrorists and all foreign imperialism. But the edited version failed to register the impact planned by Pabst since the final sequences were subverted by French censors who wanted to avoid diplomatic friction. The conclusion was rendered vague and indefinite so that the smuggling of arms seems merely an ordinary business enterprise and Tcheng's call for the revolutionary unification of the students is diluted to insignificance. During the German occupation of France, the film was banned so that its screenings were extremely limited.

Exteriors were filmed on location in Hanoi and mainland China, giving a tone of authenticity to the intrigue, and once again Schüfftan's lighting creates a mysterious quasi-Expressionist ambience appropriate to an Oriental subject. A gallery of memorable villains is provided by a talented cast: Louis Jouvet as the cynical, dessicated Ivan, with a scar across his face, and Inkijinoff, in his film debut, as a sadistic Oriental with Freudian overtones.

Before Pabst made his final pre-World-War-II film in France, he served also as supervisor on his former assistant director Marc Sorkin's film *L'Esclave Blanche* (released in the United States as *Veiled Brides*), a tale of Constantinople in 1910, starring Viviane Romance and John Lodge.

The last and the least of Pabst's French films was *Jeunes filles en détresse* (1939), written by Christa Winsloe, author of the famous *Maedchen in Uniform*, from a novel by Peter Quinn. The setting of a girl's home recalls something of *Tagebuch einer Verlorenen*, but with an emphasis on strict standards of bourgeois morality. A young girl, neglected by her parents, is sent to the institution, unaware that, like the others, she is to be the victim of a broken home. Learning of the injustice, she creates a *Ligue Contre le Divorce des Parents*, and with the help of her father, who is having an affair with her best friend's mother, she gains the support of a minister and brings about the reconciliation of her parents. In a scene that Pabst would have denounced ten years earlier, the clergyman gives a discourse on the traditional virtues of marriage. The stiflingly conventional atmosphere of *Jeunes filles en détresse* remains notable only for Pabst's use of nonprofessionals for the young girls, and for the charming presence of Micheline Presle in the central role.

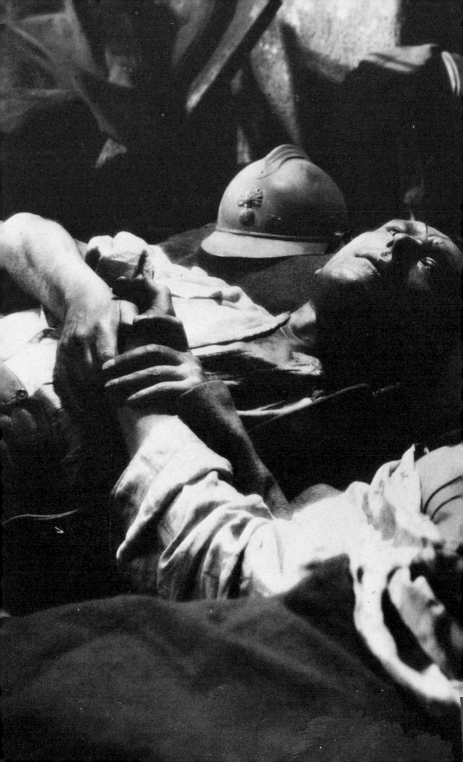

6

The Nazi Period (1941–1944)

IF PABST'S CRITICAL REPUTATION suffered considerably during his sojourn in France and the United States, it was dealt a decisive blow by his unexpected return to Nazified Austria in April, 1939. His former associates Leo Lania and Paul Falkenberg attest that Pabst had received several tempting offers, through middle men, from Goebbels urging him to return to Germany. Goebbels must have realized Pabst's difficulties but Pabst refused him each time. When he did leave for Austria, false rumors were circulated to the effect that Pabst had been a German agent in Paris and refugees throughout the world who had admired his resistance to compromise were shocked at his actions.

Pabst had in fact been the victim of circumstances and his own failure to act promptly. In a letter to the author, his wife, Gertrude Pabst, who travelled with her husband almost constantly, reveals the intricate and convincing, if unfortunate, events that led to the situation.

In 1938 Pabst already sensed the coming war. Shortly before the visit of Chamberlain to Berchtesgaden and München, we traveled for safety's sake to Basel, Switzerland, in order to wait out the affair in a neutral country. After the compromise between Chamberlain and Hitler, we returned, partly reassured, back to Paris. Then, Pabst began location filming in Saigon on *Le Drame de Shanghai*.
At the beginning of 1939, French citizenship was offered to Pabst, but as he foresaw the impending war—which he considered unavoidable—he was afraid that if he accepted citizenship his son Peter (born 1924) would be drafted into the French army and would have to fight against Germans. Although he was very much against Hitler and the Nazis, he still loved Germany. . . . He thus delayed his decision, since a direct refusal would have been insulting, though it caused him great pain. . . . Once more, we went to Switzerland, to Vevey, where we decided to emigrate to the U.S.A.

Wounded soldier in Westfront 1918

Since we had already become U.S. citizens in 1934 and would soon be in danger of losing it because of nonresidence, we had to return. Consequently, we traveled to the family estate, "Five Towers," in Southern Austria, which today has been in the Pabst-Broda family for 53 years, a beautiful and secure place in the life of the family, situated in the Steiermark region away from the war clouds of the day. The whole family assembled there to say their 'goodbyes' since we were leaving Europe, though Georg Wilhelm's aging mother was upset about our decision to emigrate to America. . . .

G. W. booked our ship passage for the 8th of September to New York (documents still exist), but on September 1st war broke out. I remember that we felt paralyzed for days, sustaining extreme shock. We remained on the estate for several weeks, then in October, we traveled to Rome to see if we could get to New York on an Italian ship and found that we could. Immediately, we traveled back to get our son, Peter, and pack our belongings. As we were preparing to depart from the train, Pabst lifted a suitcase from a luggage rack and suffered a hernia. Since the train we were on went to Vienna, we remained on it. There an immediate operation was unavoidable. . . . Even after ten days in the hospital, the incision would still not heal and the doctors discovered in retrospect a severe diabetic condition of which Pabst had not been previously aware. Seven months later, the incision had still not healed and caused painful infection which needed medical treatment every other day. Under these conditions, we could not think about travel, much less emigration to America. On top of it all, Italy had become involved in the war. G. W. complained often and was worried about what people, especially his friends, would think about him since they did not know about the unhappy circumstances in which he found himself. . . .[1]

This account is substantially confirmed by a close friend, Rudolph S. Joseph, who had also reserved passage with the Pabsts on the *Normandie,* bound for New York. Since communications were made difficult by wartime restrictions, the doubt and accusations were understandable. When Pabst's condition improved, he returned to the family estate where he remained until paid a call by Goebbels' emissaries.

When Pabst's postwar film, *Der Prozess,* found its way to American shores, Leo Lania wrote in a letter to the *New York Times:* "It is true that Pabst worked in Germany during the war. He had to. He had returned to his estate in Southern Austria, but under Nazi rule he was not permitted to remain idle. The two films he directed were historical pictures without any Nazi tinge. He neither directed nor produced propaganda films. He did not let himself be used for any glorification of the Nazi regime."[2]

Unfortunately, these blunt assertions by Lania, were, at best, half-truths. In their recent study of Pabst, Yves Aubry and Jacques Pétat assemble post-facto evidence against the director that does not stand in his favor.

1. Pabst was the only great *cinéaste* from before the war to be found in Germany at this time, all others having emigrated. His isolation thus became symbolic, more for the Nazis than for those who had chosen exile;

2. The first film he made won the Gold Medal at Venice in 1941;

3. The themes of these films correspond to the kind of propaganda wanted, independent of the anti-Semitic work directed by the Nazis.[3]

Aubry and Pétat also state that before Pabst returned to Austria he returned the Order of the Legion of Honor bestowed on him by the French government. But Mrs. Pabst emphatically denies this, claiming that Pabst, until his dying days, maintained a strong kinship with France.

Paul Rotha has suggested that Pabst had a hand in the newsreel compilation film, *Feldzug im Polen* (Baptism of Fire) (1939), and recently David Stewart Hull claims to have traced two uncredited scenes from Leni Riefenstahl's *Tiefland* to Pabst. Although we may never know the exact extent of his involvement in the Third Reich's propaganda effort, the films signed by him do correspond to a kind of entertainment genre favored by the government, glorifying Aryan cultural heroes from Germany's past. However, as we have had occasion to note, the strength of Pabst's art lay not so much in its ideological import as in its artistic merit; and far from being the uninteresting failures some writers would have us believe, *Komödianten* (1941) and *Paracelsus* (1943) confirm that, in spite of adverse political conditions, Pabst flourished best in his native environment.

Komödianten (Comedians)

Komödianten was planned and executed on a large scale, somewhat in "the Hollywood manner," and employed much of the remaining German talent in theater and cinema. Produced by Bavaria-Film in Munich, its large cast featured veteran actors Gustav Diessl and Henny Porten, and in the leading role of Karoline

Neuber, theatrical star Kathe Dorsch. In spite of the script's stuffy literary air, Pabst's talent with actors is brought to bear, along with moments of visual panache.

Komödianten follows the general trend of resurrecting historical figures and investing them with an image of heroic determinism in the face of adversity. Pabst's first "period piece" recreated major events in the life of Karoline Neuber and her eighteenth century contemporaries in a romantic style and evidences a dash of wit that would have pleased a director like Ernst Lubitsch.

The first hour, full of long stretches of arch dialogue, sets up relationships between members of Karoline's acting company and her hot-tempered disputes with Müller Hanswurst, the harlequin, whom she considers not a true actor but merely a buffoon. One of their encounters transpires in a tavern where Philine Schroeder, the *jeune première* of the company, is set upon by two old lechers. Here Pabst captures a vitality and visual atmosphere, missing from the static theatrical rehearsals and Karoline's attempts to produce a refined theatrical culture to equal that of other European countries.

The second hour proves, fortunately, more rewarding. Karoline wins the friendship and patronage of the Duchess Amalie von Weissenfels—beautifully played by a middle-aged Henny Porten —whom she persuades to institute a truly national theater in Germany. Under the wing of the duchess, Karoline is smothered in luxury and at a lavish costume party she meets the dashing and debonair Duke of Coburg, Ernst Brion, nephew to the duchess, who soon falls in love with Philine, already the object of numerous suitors. In this costumed celebration, Pabst regains some of the pictorial finesse of his earlier German work. The sequence opens on a close-up of a servant in a wine cellar selecting a bottle; he delivers it to another servant at the doorway, and with a series of rhythmic cuts, the bottle passes from one man to another up a circular staircase; and finally the camera cranes up to the rafters of a spacious ballroom, capturing a panoramic view of colorful festivities and furnishings arranged on a long dining table. One senses a momentary freedom and pleasure in this grand cinematic gesture through which Pabst enlivens a highly mannered and artificial narrative.

All goes well with plans for the new theater until the duchess, revealing her hidden prejudices against the *komödianten* (comedians), flatly refuses to allow Ernst Brion to marry young Philine, whom she considers sweet but hardly suitable as a match for the duke. Stormy theatrics ensue with Karoline displaying a Shakespearean eloquence in her defense of the marriage and Philine's honor. Offended by her manners and approach, Duchess Amalie orders Karoline banished from her homeland. In St. Petersburg, Karoline gives a performance for the court, but the audience is too accustomed to light French farce to appreciate Goethe. Discouraged and rejected, Karoline dies alone, the victim of a public that continues to support the malicious and egocentric Müller. Pabst's treatment of the courtiers of St. Petersburg reveals his special delight in detailing the customs, idiosyncrasies, and cultural prejudices of a social élite.

In the final sequence, Philine, inspired by Karoline's courage, sacrifices her love for the duke, takes up the cause where her leader failed, and succeeds in creating the first National Theater at Weimar. The strong note of patriotism in this conclusion was not unnoticed by Goebbels' Ministry of Culture, which apparently considered it to be "educationally valuable" for its chauvinistic message and its winning a prize at the Venice Biennale, then a Fascist-controlled event. Seen in the context of more rampantly nationalistic Nazi cinema, *Komödianten* today seems innocent by comparison. Beneath its powdered wigs, polite gestures, and formal verbiage, one glimpses Pabst's hand, resigned, but still active.

Paracelsus

In 1942, Goebbels proposed that Pabst make a film on the exploits of *Heinrich I, Gennant der "Vogler"* (876–936), a German ruler who re-annexed Lorraine to his kingdom and created a powerful military system to combat the Slavs. Pabst rejected the idea immediately, not giving it a second thought. The following year, however, he agreed to do a film on the mystical physician Theophrastus Bombastus von Hohenheim, known as Paracelsus (1493–1541).

Paracelsus was inspired by a historical novel, *Konig der Arzte*, by Pert Peternell, that was only remotely based on the actual facts of Paracelsus' life. In his recent book *Film and the Third Reich*, David Stewart Hull writes: "Five books about Paracelsus were published in 1941, all of them wildly nationalistic in nature, crediting him with Nazi ideals."[4] In Pabst's film, however, there is no suggestion that although Paracelsus gleaned some important medical knowledge from his encounters with Eastern magic and alchemy, he was a fanatic and charlatan who publicly burned writings of other physicians and declared himself a kind of deity. Nevertheless, whatever factual inaccuracies and distortions were introduced into Kurt Heuser's verbose screen treatment, it inspired Pabst to direct one of his most brilliant films.

The setting is Basel, during the Renaissance, recreated with richly designed costumes and settings at the Bavaria studios in Munich. Pabst is naturally drawn to the contrasting social environment. The rich entourage of Pfefferkorn, a Swiss merchant, stands out against the wretched poverty of the lower classes in the opening scene set at the entrance to a cathedral. A flirtation between the merchant's wife and Johannes Famulus, a young student, is introduced while the Schoolmaster, played by a subdued Fritz Rasp, visits an invalid who is suffering from a leg injury. Pabst intercuts shots of the poor in the streets proclaiming the miraculous healing powers of Paracelsus, while Johannes and his friends stop Renata, the merchant's wife, and chase her through the marketplace. At the same time, a woman begs entrance to Paracelsus' lodging where he is examining a young girl. A "surgeon" arrives at the home of the invalid to saw off the invalid's leg, but is restrained by Johannes, who questions the remedy. Paracelsus arrives in time to engage in a dispute with the Schoolmaster that turns the other physician away and leads to the administering of a healing potion.

This symphonic interweaving of contrasting atmospheres and narrative threads gives *Paracelsus* a distinct cinematic style and rhythm. The consistent use of Rembrandt-like chiaroscuro by Pabst's cameraman, Bruno Stephan, clothes it in a flavor of musty authenticity and beauty.

The principal conflict emerges at a debate in the town council between the Schoolmaster, who wants Paracelsus expelled from the city, and such reasoned defense as can be offered by Erasmus and Count von Hohenried. When Paracelsus speaks to the assembly of his new discoveries in hermetic medicine with passion and fervor, a contingent of youths led by Johannes comes to his support, awed at the words of the learned man. Even the Schoolmaster is impressed by his speech and the doctor continues to expound theories to Johannes and other students at the local tavern. Here we can see in Paracelsus' oratorical style something of Hitler's harangue and charisma for the German people.

When a plague threatens the city, Paracelsus, now a figure of authority, orders the town quarantined and the gates sealed.

Meanwhile, the obdurate Pfefferkorn hires men to smuggle goods into the city by night, but Paracelsus learns of the plot and has the goods burned. Later, he encounters one of the smugglers, Fliegenbein, in a local tavern. Fliegenbein, portrayed by the great dancer Harold Kreutzberg, entertains the crowd with tricks and acrobatics that soon develop into a wildly uninhibited *Totentanz* (Dance of Death), drawing the entire crowd into frenzied gyrations, climaxing in the dancer's collapse. Paracelsus discerns early symptoms of the plague on the juggler's fingers, and the crowd flees in terror, leaving only Johannes to assist Paracelsus, who embraces Fliegenbein despite his affliction. With images of epic power and intensity, Pabst films the hysterical populace forming a giant cross and flagellating themselves in a dark, open square.

Learning of her husband's treachery, Renata joins Johannes at Paracelsus' laboratory, which takes on an Expressionist aura through camera movement and lighting that creates deep shadows reflecting mysticism and adversity. The young people follow the doctor's advice and flee the city. Meanwhile, fear mounts as Paracelsus, laboring over a cure for the disease, is visited by a soldier who rightly diagnoses himself as stricken. When Ulrich von Hutten, a prominent citizen, is seized by the illness, Paracelsus administers a potion that momentarily effects a miraculous cure, but when the man dies, Paracelsus is roughly expelled. While Fliegenbein diverts the populace by walking a tightrope and flinging coins in the street, Paracelsus departs from Basel.

Even more than the previous film, *Paracelsus* was "educationally valuable" for the Reich in that its central character is symbolic of the "enlightenment" of the German leader. Its effectiveness in this respect may be surmised on the basis of the persuasive performance of Werner Krauss, whose noble features are made to resemble those in the monumental sculptures and paintings of Michelangelo and Leonardo. On the other hand, Arthur Lennig has suggested that the entire theme of the film might be interpreted as anti-Nazi and that the character of Fliegenbein might be a surrogate figure for Pabst. However we choose to view the ideological implications of the story, Pabst never allows the bombastic rhetoric to overwhelm his finely shaded baroque composition. In terms of drama and pictorial imagination, it ranks along with *Dreigroschenoper* and *Kameradschaft*.

In 1943, Pabst went to the Barrandov studios at Prague to film

Der Fall Molander, based on a novel, *Die Sternegeige* by Alfred Karrasch, reportedly about an imitation Stradivarius. Just as shooting had been completed and work had begun on editing, Prague was invaded by the Russian army and Pabst was forced to leave the film unfinished. French historians René Jeanne and Charles Ford suggest that it might have been later edited and distributed by the Russians but more recently David Stewart Hull discovered that it was destroyed in the bombing of a laboratory.

7

Trials and Tribulations (1947–1955)

AFTER THE WAR, Pabst remained in Austria where postwar difficulties were not as severe as in Germany, but opportunities for film production were few. Although his former associates Eugen Schüfftan and Leo Lania claim that he had not changed, his subsequent film work suggests that his experiences during the war—about which we know almost nothing—left a mark on his psyche from which he never fully recovered.

Defense of the Jews: *Der Prozess*

In 1933, Pabst had made known his desire to make a film about Jewish pogroms since anti-Semitic sentiments were already emanating from Germany, but he was unable to interest anyone in France in such a subject. It was strategically unfortunate that he returned to this volatile topic *after* the war, even though it inspired one of his strongest and most moving films, for the critical establishment in Germany and France was quick to denounce it, sensing a flagrant attempt by Pabst to exonerate himself for remaining silent during the Holocaust of European Jews by the Nazis. The headline for René Geneste's review in *L'Ecran Français* makes the bias clear: "Dans son nouveau film, 'Le Procès,' G. W. Pabst défend les Juifs. . . mais dix ans trop tard." More irrational observers even labelled it as anti-Semitic propaganda, pointing to the Jewish types in the film as "grotesque," and the "Christian-liberal liberator" as a contrived *deus ex machina*. Having hopefully distanced ourselves from this understandably emotional atmosphere, it is perhaps possible to view more objectively *Der Prozess* as a sincere and valid work of film art in which Pabst invested his humanist sympathy and directorial talent.

The story, taken from the novel, *Prozess auf Leben und Tod*, by Rudolf Brunngraber, transpires in late nineteenth century Hungary

131

Karl Schönböck as Carl Maria von Weber in Durch die Walder, Durch die Auen

and is based on true events in the life of a famed lawyer, Karoly
Eötvös, who became noted for his defense of the Jews.

In a small Hungarian village, where a considerable Jewish population is openly tolerated yet secretly scorned, Esther Solymosi, a
servant girl, unable to sustain harrassment by her employers,
drowns herself in a river. The suicide, not directly seen but evoca-
tively suggested, is a masterful cinematic epiphany blending a dark,
brooding painterly landscape with a crescendo of church bells, con-
veying the young girl's anguish and final surrender.

The drama's central protagonists are introduced as Peczely
Scharf, the local rabbi, leads his congregation to their synagogue.
Later, at the Scharf home, his younger son, Moritz, is reprimanded
for not attending the religious service. He rebels against his father's
stern traditionalism, declaring he has no use for his religion. Meanwhile, a night search by the girl's employer and Mrs. Solymosi
reveals no evidence of the missing Esther. That same night, her
mother in a vivid dream—rendered through a complex superim-
position of faces, voices, and shadows—is convinced that Esther has
been victimized by local Jews. When news of the dream is passed
on, the rumor spreads that Esther has been the victim of a "ritual
murder" committed by Jews, though several voices of reason pro-
claim that a dream could hardly prove such an atrocity. While ob-
serving the feast of the Passover with family and friends, the Rabbi
Scharf is deeply disturbed at the accusation.

News of the incident reaches Budapest, where Bary, an ambitious
and unscrupulous official, is assigned to investigate the matter. The
villagers testify that neither Salomon Schwartz, a moneylender dismissed by Baron Onody, nor young Moritz can account for their
activities at the time of the girl's disappearance, and both are sum-
marily arrested. During the course of interrogation, Bary realizes
that young Scharf, while he offers no acceptable story, is opposed to
his father's faith. Following sleepless nights of constraint and mental
exhaustion. Moritz breaks down and signs a declaration stating that
he, as well as other Jews, joined in killing the girl. Consequently, all
the Jews in the village are ordered under arrest and, with the open
expression of anti-Jewish feeling in the air, Gentiles of the community burn the local synagogue.

In Budapest, Both, a sensitive young lawyer, is assigned to prose-
cute the case, though he privately denounces the whole affair as a
scandalous provocation, unsupportable in a court of law. Torn be-

tween duty and conscience, he ultimately commits suicide. When the Nationalists demand a trial of the Jews, an opposition party is organized by Baron Onody to hire Dr. Eötvös and expose the truth. Meanwhile, young Moritz is surrendered to the custody of the police commissioner and soon becomes infatuated with his daughter. A representative of the Anti-Semitic Congress arrives at the Solymosi home offering them money, an offer quickly withdrawn as word arrives that Esther's body has been recovered from the river. Mrs. Solymosi, refusing to believe that her daughter would take her life, declines to identify the corpse.

Fearing exposure, Bary and his aid, Egressy, torture several villagers, hoping to extract a confession to prove the body was a substitution. Contrasting with the inquisitional agony, Pabst stages a costume ball at which Bary, the commissioner, and his associates mingle with society. Glimpses of the screaming victims of Bary's men alternate with Moritz romancing the commissioner's daughter at the ball; cornered by guests about the crime, he is rescued by Dr. Eötvös, whose own questions expose the fallacy of their inquiry.

The tribunal moves swiftly over the salient points of the case while Pabst builds the ominous progression with low-angle compositions, shafts of window light, and counterpoints the legal oratory with reactions of jury and the accused, as well as the conspirators. When the court refuses to accept proof of a murder having been committed, Mrs. Solymosi recounts the revelations of her dream, but a servant offers persuasive evidence that Esther ended her own life. A victim of persistent "brain-washing," young Moritz testifies to the contrary, however, in a carefully coached recital prompted by the prosecution. When confronted by a plea from his emotionally overcome father, the boy renounces all his ties with Judaism in a moment of shattering dramatic impact.

The *pièce de résistance,* however, is provided by a reconstruction of the crime, avowed to have taken place in the village synagogue. The smoky charred remnants of the building are a carefully composed setpiece of angular geometric distortions, reviving the remnants of a Caligariesque Expressionism and are the plastic equivalents of the vicious conspiracy. Only through this extreme measure and insisting that Bary act out the role of the murderer is Eötvös able to prove conclusively that the entire case is a racist-inspired hoax.

The summation of the argument for the defense is conveyed

Procession and synagogue scenes from Der Prozess. *Top: Ernst Deutsch as the rabbi.*

through fragments, connected by emphatic music. Though Eötvös is unequivocal in denouncing the shameful prejudice involved—"Our hatred is not the result of reason, but rather the result of a conviction!"—his subsequent reasoning—"I defend them not because they are Jews, but because I am a Christian"—made Pabst vulnerable to criticism. The film's most emotionally moving and powerfully etched moment occurs in the reconciliation between the rabbi—beautifully conceived by Ernst Deutsch—and his young son, though the finale is marred by an "inspirational" shot in which the liberated Jews march into a bright ray of light, accompanied by a soaring chorus and orchestra.

Festival prizes are never any guarantee of quality, yet it is noteworthy that *Der Prozess* was awarded two at the Venice Festival in 1948; to Pabst for best direction, and to Ernst Deutsch for best performance by an actor. These did not, however, pave the way for international accolades. The premiere was in Zürich, Switzerland, and screenings in Germany were limited to *ciné-clubs* in Berlin and Hamburg. While rancorous ethnic attitudes may still persist over *Der Prozess*, its sustained beauty, visual imagination, and deeply felt characterizations remain a testament to Pabst's creative powers and to his humanist concern for the Jewish people who had so grievously suffered under Hitler.

Having acknowledged the excellence of *Der Prozess*, one must concede that it marks the beginning of a regressive, even conservative trend in Pabst's career. In his postwar films he deals almost exclusively with a literary or historic past. Identifying with the class in which he was born and its prejudices, he became unable to confront the social problems of a society that had supported to the end Hitler and his crimes against humanity. As Guido Aristarco has argued, Pabst reduces the postwar experience to a vague conflict between good and evil, in which evil is identified with the present and good only with the past. In fact, the former advocate of social realism moved increasingly toward a position of mysticism or romantic evasion.

Italian Interlude

In 1949, Pabst formed his own production company in Vienna, Pabst-Kiba Filmproduktion, under the auspices of which he supervised the work of three other directors: Paul May (*Duell Mit Dem Tod*), Hubler-Kahla (*1-2-3 Aus!*), and Georg C. Klaren (*Ruf Aus Dem Äther*). May's *Duel with Death*, co-authored by Pabst, is of

interest since it concerns an anti-Nazi professor who escapes a
prison sentence and in the Tyrol helps liberate prisoners during the
war. But the one film directed by Pabst himself during this period,
Geheimnisvolle Tiefen, from a story by Pabst's wife and Walter
Hollander, was pure romantic escapism and reverts to the manner
of his least typical silent films, *Der Schatz* and *The White Hell of
Pitz-Palü*. In a remote section of the Pyrenees, a young scientist,
while involved in a dangerous geological excavation, is deserted by
his fiancée for a wealthy industrialist. Hearing he is endangered,
she returns to him and they are trapped together in a cavern. The
industrialist comes to rescue them but she remains with the scientist whom she now knows she loves. Pabst's rather weak, melodramatic defense of love, triumphing over a mediocre bourgeois
marriage, is unconvincing, though his penchant for Expressionist
décor is once again evidenced.

Geheimnisvolle Tiefen, in spite of its artistic pretentions enjoyed
no commercial success. As a result Pabst once again considered
working abroad. By 1950, he had completed a script based on
Homer's epic *The Odyssey* and had dreams of directing it in English
as a co-production, with Gregory Peck in the starring role and Greta
Garbo in the triple role of Penelope, Circe, and Calypso. During a
brief excursion to New York, he presented the script to the now
reclusive Garbo for consideration. When she failed to give him an
answer, Pabst departed for Italy where he was invited to stage
operas in Florence and Verona, and where he directed two oddly
untypical and uninspired films.

The first of these was a French-English-Italian co-production, *La
Voce del Silenzio* (The Voice of Silence) (1952), based on an idea of
Cesare Zavattini, one of the Italian cinema's most prestigious advocates of social realism. The final scenario, boasting thirteen credited
writers (including Jean Cocteau, presumably explaining Jean
Marais' inclusion in the cast), was a mélange of half-baked neo-
realism and sentimental comedy-drama, given a rather heavy, often
indifferent treatment by Pabst, notwithstanding some outstanding
visual qualities.

A collection of diverse types retreat, for varied reasons, to a Jesuit
convent in Rome for a period of quiet soul-searching and spiritual
renewal. There is a candlemaker who goes out of family tradition
and for business reasons; a thief, who is in flight with stolen jewels; a
novelist, who has been on trial for printing a scandalous book; a

priest, who is suffering a crisis of conscience and wants to forsake his vows; and a partisan, whose wife believes him dead, and who suffers from the memory of having caused the death of three innocent children in the war. Some decide to stay for the designated period, others realize they are fleeing from reality and leave.

Pabst might have been attracted to the story through identifying with several of the characters, and the enigmatic title itself suggests something of his mental state in regard to the past. He may have seen something of himself in the novelist who recalls the noble sentiments with which he began his career and then gradually was led to sell out his principles. The novelist's past encounter with a lawyer is set in a Roman tavern, in deep shadow and given a distorted appearance by a wide-angle lens that recalls Pabst's Expressionist manner. Similarly, Pabst's camera is as fluid as ever in a night sequence where a young girl (Rossana Podesta) is forced to strip for a gang in a catacomb, but the quality of the acting by his international cast is fitful and generally indifferent, with only Daniel Gélin and Jean Marais registering any emotional depth. Most impressive are the dream memories of Marais as the partisan, with flashes of brief marital bliss alternating with vivid war scenes in which the children and an old man are caught in a fatal bridge explosion.

Cosi da Pazzi (Crazy Affairs), a second Italian venture in 1953, reunited Pabst with his former scenarist Leo Lania and was planned as a satire on modern civilization's tendency to produce psychopathology. It originated in a story by Bruno Paolinelli (who had assisted Pabst in mounting his Verdi operas) that sounds quite diverting. A young girl, through a misunderstanding, is mistakenly diagnosed as insane and sent to an asylum where she is barely able to distinguish the inmates from the keepers. The institution is operated by a kind of contemporary dictator whose methods are emulated by a co-worker who finally falls in love with the girl. Pabst's treatment of it was, unhappily, not successful and Italian critics and audiences found its humor rather heavy-handed and labored.

Pabst's Italian excursion proved almost as unfruitful as his Hollywood venture and soon convinced him to return to Germany to direct his first film there since the war. In *Das Bekenntnis der Ina Kahr*, Pabst returns to the battle of the sexes, but without any subtlety or grace. This exercise in routine melodrama about an unfaithful husband (Curt Jurgens) who is killed by his wife

138   G. W. PABST

(Elisabeth Müller), marks the nadir of Pabst's postwar career, suggesting that he had fallen permanently into the quagmire of mediocrity that distinguished most German films of the time. But he was to rise once more from defeat and create one more master-work worthy of his name.

Shadows of Hitler: *Der Letzte Akt* and *Es Geschah am 20 Juli*

The mediocrity of Pabst's postwar work might be explained by the low quality of German film production in general, but, in fact, his excursions to America and Italy were evasive diversions from a subject he had been preoccupied with since the end of the war: a film about Hitler. Hitler had already been impersonated in many dramatic films by such actors as Ludwig Donath (*The Strange Death of Adolf Hitler*, 1943), Robert Watson (*The Hitler Gang*, 1944), Luther Adler (*The Magic Face*, 1951), and in satiric style by Chaplin in *The Great Dictator*. In German film, however, a trend was formulated—exemplified by Alfred Weidemann's popular *Admiral Canaris*—that camouflaged guilt complexes by accusing Hitler of everything and trying to prove that all Germans were not Nazi.

Pabst was determined that his image would be unsparing in its truthfulness and that it would capture the atmosphere of collective paranoia that found its central focus in the dementia of the Führer himself whose insidious thinking spawned a nationalist conspiracy. He ultimately found a treatment that appealed to him in Erich Maria Remarque's scenario, taken from the journal of Michael A. Musmano of the International Tribunal at Nuremberg, *Ten Days to Die*. The final script, written by Fritz Habeck, remains close to documentation with only a few additions for dramatic purposes.

Pabst proceeded to cast the film with extreme care, choosing actors who not only closely physically resembled their real counter-parts but who were also skilled actors. Hitler's bunker was com-pletely reconstructed according to its original size and layout on the sound stage. Pabst was determined to realign himself, aesthetically, with his former "realist" tendencies, with an unadorned vision of a claustrophobic environment.

Known in Britain as *Ten Days to Die* and in the U.S. as *The Last Ten Days*, *Der Letzte Akt* unravels the events that reportedly occur-red in and around the Chancellery in Berlin during the last days of the Führer's reign of terror. For the most part, Pabst remains in this closely guarded arena, studying the deterioration of Hitler, psychologically and physically, as a metaphor for the impending collapse of an entire nation. The most significant concession to fiction is the figure of Wurst, a young captain, splendidly portrayed by Oskar Werner, who gradually comes to represent the spirit of humanistic conscience tragically caught in a web of insanity. Functioning as a chorus of one, he is the first and last person to appear on screen. Initially, he is carrying out orders to accompany an officer on a special mission. When the officer is killed, he hopes to take his place and reports to the Führer himself but his request is consistently turned down.

Unaware that Wurst has arrived with news from the Eastern front, Hitler continues to argue with his generals over military strategy, refusing to consider the situation rationally. Like a medieval monarch he consults his astrologer, who naturally forecasts victory. When his closest advisors salute him on his birthday, then advise him that he is no longer safe in Berlin, Hitler responds with a defensive rage and personally assumes total control of his military machine. The staunch idealism of his youngest soldiers is evidenced in a brief, perfectly realized scene in which the Führer decorates a group of teen-age boys for bravery and smilingly stuffs them with cake and coffee, while from a beer hall replete with Pabstian "atmosphere" men are called from drinking and singing to defend the city.

In addition to the fictional introduction of Captain Wurst, Pabst follows briefly the peregrinations of a young soldier on leave to visit his family. These scenes not only provide relief from the highly charged atmosphere of Hitler's Chancellery but also comment on the sinking morale and deflated illusions of the average German. The boy is traumatized by the suicide of a defeated major who hangs himself from a lamppost, and while searching for his bedridden mother, the youth ends up in a subway station that has been temporarily coverted into a hospital for the scores of wounded.

Having established the various themes and subjects, Pabst proceeds to develop them through alternating contrast until they reach a climax in the finale. Wurst ultimately succeeds in gaining an audience with Hitler to reveal the failing German position at the front, but the leader willfully consolidates his forces against the Americans and Russians. While Wurst drowns his fears in a beer hall, Hitler retreats to his private sanctuary where he momentarily contemplates suicide. Then, overwhelmed by a moment of transcendent visionary madness, he sees the earth as a filthy swamp filled with "slimy beasts," and yearns for a single weapon with which he might obliterate everything, calling on the spirit of his predecessor, Frederick the Great.

Fears of betrayal by everyone are accentuated after Wurst is assigned to bunker operations. Goering is ordered under arrest when he sends the Führer an ultimatum warning of impending disaster. Even as an officer on an operating table confides to him that the Fatherland is lost, Hitler stubbornly persists with his illusion of victory in this "black hour." Facing the bunker alone, he is sensitive to the slightest infraction, even accusing Himmler of betrayal.

The dramatic climax is provided by the invasion of Berlin and Hilter's decision to flood the subway tunnels under Friedrichstrasse to slow the Allied assault on the city. Now the German leader resembles a mere husk of a man, hounded by fear and heedless of the wounded in the underground ("What is another thousand or more now?"). While the boy whose mother is endangered begs Wurst to intercede, Pabst intercuts a brief scene in which two officers privately voice their fears of what will happen to them when "all this" is over. The beginning of the end is announced as Wurst confronts the solitary and terror-stricken Führer in his private quarters with the monstrosity of his act and the quiet affirmation that "a man shouldn't always obey orders." Cornering his leader in a stranglehold, Wurst is fatally wounded by guards.

Pabst plays off the anxiety-ridden atmosphere of the bunker against the flooding of the subway with great virtuosity and power in composition and editing tempo. While Hitler and Eva Braun are married in a brief, solemn ceremony, and Wurst is slowly dying in the arms of a young soldier, in the smoke-filled beer cellar men and women dance and drink themselves into oblivion and erotic embrace as hundreds of victims are trapped by the onrush of water in the underground tunnels. Following the death of Hitler and his bride—aurally indicated by off-screen gunfire heard by the staff in an ajoining room—Pabst cuts to a long silent tracking through the water-logged tunnel revealing no signs of life. The bodies of Hitler and Eva Braun are incinerated in a shallow ditch, and overlapping with a shot of the flames is a close-up of the expiring Wurst whose last words summon the Hitlerian youth to surrender: "Always keep the faith, never say *Jawohl*, that's how it all began."

Wurst's final words, implicating everyone in Hitler's conspiracy, not just his bloodthirsty henchmen and cowardly assistants, but everyone who saluted the cause, failed to win the approval of German audiences and critics, though opinion elsewhere was unanimously positive; and Pabst's last masterpiece graced the Locarno and Edinburg festivals where it acquired an international distribution, the first in many years for a Pabst film.

Pabst's dramatic and imaginative portrayal of this tragic episode in German history derives its efficacy to a large degree not from fidelity to historical fact but from its poetic and psychological intensity rendered through fluid cinematic techniques. By lighting and shooting from low angles, often exposing the very low ceilings of the sets, Pabst accentuates the claustrophobic atmosphere of the bunker, and the constant play of light and shadow becomes increasingly menacing as the action draws to its climactic stages. Flexible settings allow the camera an expressive mobility and while the textures of the photography are relatively free from Pabst's early Expressionist embellishments, the scenes in the beer halls and the flooded subway naturally bear a resemblence to moments in *Pandora's Box* and *Kameradschaft*.

The direction of the actors is uniformly inspired. All other impersonations of Hitler—including succeeding ones by Richard Basehart and Alec Guinness—remain caricatures beside the veracity of Albin Skoda's, for which he achieved fame. Not only does a skilled makeup transform him into a close match for Hitler, but his uncanny ability to duplicate his vocal and physical mannerisms and modulate emotional ranges from paternal affection to sudden rage to boiling fury are conveyed with astonishing finesse and power, without falling into melodramatic cliché. Equally distinguished in this respect are Willy Krauss's Goebbels and Eric Suckmann's Heinrich Himmler.

Pabst gives special attention, however, to Oskar Werner's character. Although it might be argued that the film's thesis could have been conveyed equally well without him and that fictional license robs his role of authenticity, nevertheless, he embodies the sentiments of a director who needed a surrogate figure to represent his own conscience in a final effort to clear himself. Out of the nightmare of a recent past, Pabst's creation registered a powerful truth that exposed the shallow pomp and artificiality of earlier efforts like Rajzman's *The Fall of Berlin* (USSR, 1947). At the same time, Albin

Skoda's portrait of Hitler can be seen as a successor to Werner Krauss's Dr. Caligari, confirming the psychological evolution traced in German cinema by Siegfried Kracauer (*From Caligari to Hitler*).

Pleased with the success of *Der Letzte Akt*, Pabst began work immediately on a companion film, *Es Geschah am 20 Juli*, about the unsuccessful attempt of army officers, under Colonel Count Stauffenberg, to seize control of power from Hitler. Pabst viewed the plot as symbolic of the resistance from within of the German people. The scheme begins in July 1944, when the people and the army of the Reichland, beaten at home and in the field, continue to resist only under the threat of governmental orders. Hitler's failure as a leader draws together the opponents of his regime, including a powerful group of officers who were once part of the German Imperial Army. Stauffenberg, believing that Hitler's irrational acts will ruin Germany, prepares a plot to assassinate him by planting a bomb in his headquarters. After the explosion on July 20, Stauffenberg returns to Berlin, believing Hitler is dead and confident that his fellow conspirators had taken action to arrest the chiefs of the Nazi party; but failure of the code words "operation over" to reach General Olbricht prevents the plan from going into effect. Step by step, Pabst uncovers the small miscalculations that build to a general confusion as Remer, learning that Hitler is alive, does not arrest Goebbels, but pretends to help him. The Army Signals play it safe by transmitting both the orders of the conspirators and those from Hitler's East Prussia headquarters until they are certain the plot has failed. The net closes around the officers as their orders to the Army fail to be executed and Stauffenberg realizes that the former glory of the Imperial Army he had hoped to revive was already dead before Hitler's accession to power.

Unfortunately, during shooting of the film, Pabst was forced to double time to keep pace with another company producing a film on the identical subject as his own. The result was two mediocre films instead of one. Concentrating on the complex mechanism of the plot, Pabst and his technicians were unable to give proper attention to details in atmosphere and characterization that make the preceding film such a powerful experience. Bernard Wicki's impersonation of Stauffenberg is often skillful in the opening scenes; but, though the casting otherwise is not inept, the other characterizations are superficial, subordinated to the manipulations of narrative, through which a certain degree of suspense is generated. Little of Pabst's creative imagination is evidenced, however.

Perhaps it would be tactful to end here this introduction to Pabst's work, although he directed two more films the following year, both commercial romantic pieces of the sort he himself proclaimed the baneful mainstay of modern German cinema (since having undergone a radical and fruitful transformation in the hands of a new generation headed by Rainer W. Fassbinder, Werner Herzog, and Volker Schlondorff). The first was *Rosen für Bettina* that unveiled the tribulations of a ballerina, stricken with poliomyelitis, who loses her lover and choreographer, to another dancer who replaces her. Despairing, she attempts suicide but is made to forget the choreographer by a doctor, whose attentive care restores her will to live and love. The second was *Durch die Walder, Durch die Auen*, about the romantic adventures of nineteenth-century composer Carl Maria von Weber, which is distinguished mostly for being Pabst's one use of color cinematography. A subject that might possibly have inspired a great film from Max Ophüls proved to be a stiff academic exercise in the hands of Pabst. A creative personality who seemed to have lost his touch, Pabst continued to work, to declare his unbounded confidence in the future of cinema as a medium that could help us transcend national differences, even though in his final years of intermittent illness the subjects he most cherished and wanted to bring to life were from the German theater repertory he had directed on the stage a half century earlier: Shiller's *Fiesko* (which was to have starred the well-known German actor O. W. Fischer) and Lessing's *Nathan der Weise* (planned for Ernst Deutsch, the star of *Der Prozess*). Pabst also had planned a film based on the biblical story of Judith. None of these went beyond planning stages.

In 1956 Pabst began to suffer as a result of his diabetes, since he was not strong enough to observe the necessarily strict diet required, and in 1957 he developed Parkinson's disease. His condition was further complicated by cerebral arteriosclerosis, rendering him an invalid for the remaining decade of his life. On May 29, 1967, after contracting an acute liver infection, Pabst died in Vienna at the age of 82.

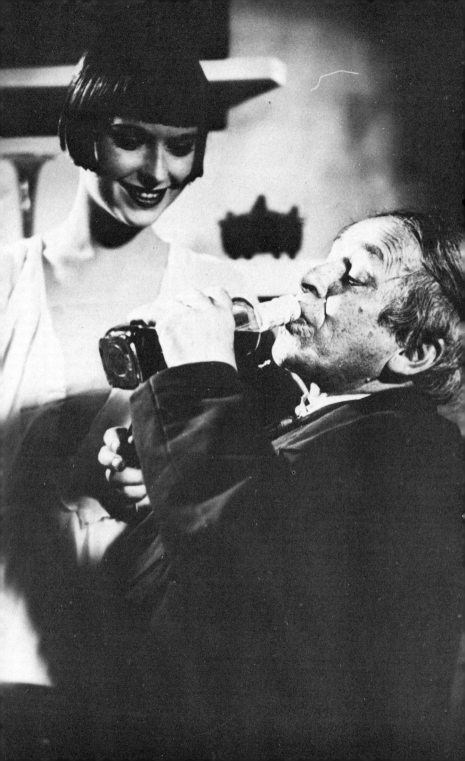

8

The Style is the Man

HERBERT LUFT, one of the last persons to interview Pabst before his death, characterized him as one of the cinema's "last individualists." Toward the end of his long and productive career the contradictions in this individualism became increasingly apparent, but in his early years Pabst inspired respect, admiration, and love from all those who knew and worked with him. Renoir, the great French humanist director who shared much in common with Pabst, as late as 1963 proclaimed him a master. "He knows how to create a strange world, whose elements are borrowed from daily life. Beyond this precious gift, he knows how, better than anyone else, how to direct actors. His characters emerge like his own children, created from fragments of his own heart and mind."[1]

While Renoir speaks from his humanist sympathies, the eminent French film historian Jean Mitry, discussing Pabst's *Die Freudlose Gasse*, finds in it the major qualities and faults that were to characterize all of Pabst's work: "An incomparable mastery in the art of creating atmosphere and a social climate; a flagrant incapacity to deal with political and social problems other than through the individual or the couple; an anarchistic ethic and a bourgeois humanism nearer that of Proudhon or Gustav Landauer than that of Karl Marx."[2] Mitry's evaluation, although colored by an ideological bias, contains much truth while at the same time it suggests the difficulty of drawing an objective portrait of the man and his work.

Pabst undoubtedly possessed a sharp and inquiring mind and eye, allied with, according to Alexandre Arnoux, "a Viennese charm that nobody I know can resist, an extraordinary power of seduction; the demon of intelligence in his look and a certain fullness and direct humanity that pierces the soul, evoking a sympathy . . . ."[3] His long-time assistant Marc Sorkin recalls that although he required discipline from his actors and crew, Pabst was always open to

145

Creating a strange world: Carl Goetz and Louise Brooks in Die Büchse der Pandora the ideas of everyone on the set, with whom he would engage in frank, open discussion, though he always retained a clear idea of what he wanted to achieve artistically. Louise Brooks, who has written most perceptively about her experiences with Pabst, describes him as "a short man, broad-shouldered and thick-chested, looking heavy and willful in repose. But in action his legs carried him on wings which matched the swiftness of his mind. He always came on the set, fresh as a March wind, going directly to the camera to check the set-up, after which he turned to his cameraman Gunther Krampf, who was the only person on the film to whom he gave a complete account of the scene's action and meaning."[4] At the same time, Brooks recalls the director's forensic skill was such that he could argue both sides of a political or social issue with equal persuasion, leaving her in doubt as to his personal convictions.

Like Griffith, Pabst viewed the cinema as a potent weapon that, in the hands of a persuasive artist, could improve social and political conditions, a position still somewhat questionable even today. In the 1930s, when he openly advocated a Marxist humanism, he stated that if he had gotten an earlier start, he would have taken up the "Kino-Eye" documentary approach of the young Russian director Dziga Vertov (an inspiration for later radical cinéastes like Jean-Luc Godard), but Pabst's ties with fictional stylization were too strong. Though deeply moved by his early experiences with the working class in America and a period of confinement in a prisoner-of-war camp in France to take up a revolutionary cause, Pabst was never able to liberate himself totally from his Austrian middle-class background and cultural conditioning. His wanderings over the urban centers of Europe, North America, and Asia gave him valuable insight into other values and social systems, but he was never able to escape his own past. "Of all German directors," writes Henri Langlois, "Pabst, who passed for the least German of them, and who in his time personified Europe, was in reality one who was unable to escape from Berlin and an atmosphere and class to which he belonged; he needed them before his camera. In spite of his talent, sensibility, and culture, his art was too vulnerable to be deprived of all this."[5] (In passing, we might note that a similar phenomenon can be observed today in the dislocation of a major film director like Michelangelo Antonioni.)

During the 1920s and early 1930s, British critics John Grierson, Paul Rotha, and Roger Manvell, impressed by the realism of the early films, along with their French contemporaries, hailed Pabst as one of the great film directors, destined to rank along with Griffith and Eisenstein. However, following a period of "social conclusiveness," culminating in 1931, the political edge becomes increasingly vague, then virtually disappears in Pabst's films. As his career progressed, the "Red Pabst" began to confound expectations with commercial, atmospheric melodramas, and estimations of his place in the pantheon of great directors were revised.

What these critics were unwilling to accept was, first, that Pabst's strength as a director was not ideological and, second, that while pursuing a new vein of realism, he remained temperamentally still profoundly romantic. Pabst is often quoted as having said, "what need is there for romanticism? Reality is already far too romantic and disconcerting." Shaped by the themes, imagery, and psychology of Expressionism, the inner distortions of which were the last desperate responses of romanticism to an increasingly dehumanized world, Pabst's phrasing sums up an evasive, dialectical rationalization of the opposing forces within his own character and artistic personality on which he founded his art.

The fluctuation between Expressionism, Impressionism, and realism, even within a single film, makes it difficult to formulate any sustained critical approach to Pabst's work. We have noted recurring visual motifs, camera angles, atmospheres and settings, social and erotic themes in surveying his output, and these might lead one to suspect a case for *auteurism* might be constructed here. In France, where there exists a general tendency to regard any great director as an *auteur* and to elaborate a justification, however tendentious, for the theory, Barthélemy Amengual has attempted a rudimentary, but unconvincing structural analysis of Pabst. The mythical and psychic significance of objects such as mirrors and clothing is related to the heritage of Expressionism and the *Kammerspielfilm,* and a brief note on Pabst's penchant for close detail is not without interest, but Amengual's analysis fails to clarify any overall motivating factors in the director's visual sensibility. For instance, Pabst returns often to the milieu of the tavern or cabaret. In *Jeanne Ney* it expresses the atmosphere of decadence incarnated in the character of Fritz Rasp; in *Abwege*, it symbolizes the heroine's psychological turmoil; in *Dreigroschenoper* and *Kameradschaft* it represents an environment of conviviality and social communion, bringing together varied social strata.

Pabst was drawn to some of the most imposing subjects and personalities of his time: postwar inflationary Vienna, the Russian Rev-

Expressionism (top) in the realistic Freudlose Gasse *(1925) and realism (bottom) in the romantic* Durch die Walder, Durch die Auen *(1956)*

olution, Freudian psychoanalysis, Wedekind, Brecht, Hitler. With each new film, however, his restless sensibility sought a fresh approach; thus each work must be judged according to its merits, while viewed in the context of an erratic creative development. Some directors such as Renoir, Griffith, Buñuel, Ford, and Lang are clearly guided by an innate personal philosophy expressed through a language and stylistic tendency maintained throughout their careers. Others, like Pabst, are more influenced by external than by internal factors, and as a result their work resists any sustained, systematic analysis. Amengual, in fact, strongly suggests this in his appraisal of his subject's vision. "Intuitive, instinctive, receptive, Pabst attaches himself to living in the world, his world, much better than he thinks about it. The meaning of detail, the intensity of his perception, emerges like a return to the fresh perceptivity of childhood. . . ."[6]

The special intuitive, instinctive quality that Pabst brought to the cinema was perhaps most brilliantly exercised in his ability to find the actors for his films. "If there was any pattern at all to Pabst's interest in his choice of stories," observes James Card, "it was obvious . . . that his field was psychology rather than sociology, his concern more with the battle of the sexes than the struggle of the classes. In five out of seven of the films Pabst had directed by 1928, the dominant protagonist was a woman."[7] Certainly, his frank and honest depiction of eroticism and sexual relationships went far beyond any of his contemporaries and his special talent with women brought to the screen a new and provocative perception of feminine psychology. Paul Rotha found it especially significant that "in each of his succeeding films, he has sought more and more to express the motives that lie behind a woman's impulsive thoughts and actions. He appears to have the power of discovering a hidden quality in an actress, whatever her career may have been before she came under his direction. Like Greta Garbo—Asta Nielsen, Edith Jehanne, Brigitte Helm, Hertha von Walther, and Louise Brooks are almost ordinary when appearing in other films under other directors. But Pabst has an understanding, an appreciation of the intelligence, that builds the actual personality into a magnetic filmic being."[8] Curiously enough, this psychological preoccupation with woman disappears almost entirely after Pabst's memorable but brief association with Louise Brooks and Brigitte Helm, and though he deals with female characters in films like *Das Bekenntnis der Ina Kahr* and

Rosen für Bettina, these qualities are not present in the performances of Elisabeth Müller. In fact, the memorable protagonists in the later part of Pabst's career are largely male, from Mackie Messer to Paracelsus and Hitler.

Pabst's method with actors was highly individualized. With trained actors such as Werner Krauss or Gustav Diessl he would offer detailed instructions, but with more instinctive, natural performers like Louise Brooks or Garbo he would explain situations and let them draw upon their own personalities and resources to create the role. With technicians he was very exacting, particularly regarding qualities of the image. Marc Sorkin testifies to the fact that compared to other directors, Pabst worked quickly, was well prepared, and always knew precisely what he wanted. "But he was also meticulous: if he wanted a particular angle, he would take a day to prepare a shot. . . . He always shot for the editor: he knew the effect he wanted before he shot the scene."[9]

The technique of cutting-on-movement which Pabst developed under the influence of the Russian montage of Eisenstein and Pudovkin in his silent films failed, however, to evolve into an expressive technique of any consequence in his later sound films in which camera movement and mise-en-scène increasingly take precedence over editing patterns. This is probably why his later work has more of a realistic feel than his earlier films, in which the plastic effect of individual shots is more pronounced.

In a contemporary perspective it seems that Pabst has not been simply underrated as a director as much as he has not been sufficiently rated at all. Like all the great cinéastes, he produced his share of potboilers and artistic lapses. His career as well as his life is full of complex motivations and inconsistencies, but this did not prevent him from giving life to a number of important films that deserve the well-worn labels of "classic" or "masterpiece." The achievement of cinema would be smaller without *Die Freudlose Gasse, Die Liebe Der Jeanne Ney, Die Büchse der Pandora*, and *Kameradschaft*. His best work reflects the constantly shifting currents of the psychological, political, and aesthetic thought of his era, and if he failed to inscribe in it a classical *Weltanschauung*, his films reflect a vibrant *Zeitgeist* and a diverse humanistic perspective that deserve recognition.

Notes and References

Preface

1. Henri Agel, *Les Grandes cinéastes* (Paris, 1959), p. 134.

Chapter One

1. Lotte H. Eisner, *The Haunted Screen* (Berkeley, 1969), p. 172.
2. Freddy Buache, "G. W. Pabst," *Premier Plan* No. 39 (Lyons, 1965), p. 7.

Chapter Two

1. Gustav F. Hartlaub, "Zür Einfuhrung," *Die neue Sachlichkeit* (Dresden, 1925), Introduction, unpaginated.
2. Yves Aubry and Jacques Pétat, "G. W. Pabst," *Anthologie du Cinéma* (Paris, 1968), 4:320.
3. Barthélmy Amengual, "George Wilhelm Pabst," *Cinéma d'Aujourd'hui* No. 37 (Paris, 1966), p. 28.
4. Arthur Lennig, "The Joyless Street," unpublished essay.
5. Paul Rotha, *The Film Till Now*, third edition (New York, 1967), pp. 268–69.
6. Siegfried Kracauer, *From Caligari to Hitler* (Princeton, 1947), p. 176.

Chapter Three

1. Marc Sorkin, "Six Talks on G. W. Pabst," *Cinemages* 3 (New York, 1955), p. 37.
2. Louise Brooks, "Mr. Pabst," *Image* 5, vii (September 1956), 154.
3. Louise Brooks, *Der Regisseur: G. W. Pabst* (München, 1963), unpaginated.
4. Louise Brooks, "Mr. Pabst," p. 155.
5. A. Kraszna-Krausz, "G. W. Pabst's *Lulu*," *Close Up* 4, iv (April 1929), 29.
6. Eisner, p. 300.
7. Kraszna-Krausz, p. 27.

8. Kracauer, p. 110–11

9. Eisner, pp. 306–07.

10. Buache, p. 46.

11. Ibid., p. 47.

12. Henri Langlois, quoted by James Card, "The Intense Isolation of Louise Brooks," *Sight and Sound* 27:241.

13. Ibid., p. 244.

14. Ibid., p. 242.

Chapter Four

1. Quoted by Amengual, p. 95.

2. Kracauer, p. 234.

3. Anon., "Skandal um Eva," *Close Up* (September 1930), 221–22.

4. Walter Weideli, *The Art of Bertolt Brecht* (New York, 1963), p. 25.

5. Leo Lania, "Six Talks on G. W. Pabst," *Cinemages* 3, p. 73.

6. Eisner, p. 343.

7. Ibid., p. 317.

8. Parker Tyler, *Classics of the Foreign Film* (New York, 1962), p. 67.

9. Harry Alan Potamkin, "Pabst and the Social Film," *Hound and Horn* 6 (January–March, 1933), 297.

10. Alan Stanbrook, "Great Films of the Century, No. 10, *Die Dreigroschenoper*," *Films and Filming* 7, vii (April 1961), 38.

11. Arlene Croce, "The Threepenny Opera," *Film Quarterly* 6, i (Fall, 1960), p. 45.

12. Kracauer, p. 241.

Chapter Five

1. Aubry and Pétat, p. 350.

2. Tyler, p. 80.

3. Lino del Fra and Tito Guerrini, "Vita e morte dell'hidalgo," quoted in Amengual, p. 19, from *Filmcritica* 34–35 (March–April, 1954).

5. G. W. Pabst interviewed by Louis Gerbe, "Les idées de Pabst sur le cinéma," *Je suis partout* 462 (Jan. 19, 1933), quoted in Amengual, p. 92.

6. Henri Langlois, *Der Regisseur: G. W. Pabst* (München, 1963), unpaginated.

7. Quoted by Amengual, p. 95, from *Le Rôle intellectuel du Cinéma* (Paris, 1937).

8. Buache, p. 88.

9. Ibid.

Chapter Six

1. Gertrude Pabst to Lee Atwell, September 13, 1976, excerpted by Lee Atwell. Translated by Elfreide Fischinger and William Moritz.

2. Leo Lania, "In Defense of Pabst," *New York Times*, April 2, 1950, X,4.

3. Aubry and Pétat, p. 361.

4. David Stewart Hull, *Film in the Third Reich* (Berkeley, 1969), p. 246.

Chapter Eight

1. Quoted in Amengual, p. 151.

2. Jean Mitry, *Histoire du cinéma: Art et industrie, III, 1923–1930* (Paris, 1973), p. 226.

3. Alexandre Arnoux, "Un déjeuner avec Pabst," *Pour Vous* 115 (January 29, 1931), in Amengual, p. 10.

4. Louise Brooks, "Pabst and Lulu," *Sight and Sound* 34 (Summer 1965), 126.

5. Henri Langlois, *Der Regisseur: G. W. Pabst,* unpaginated.

6. Amengual, p. 85.

7. James Card, "Out of Pandora's Box," *Image* 5 (September 1956), 151.

8. Rotha, p. 269.

9. Sorkin, p. 37.

Bibliography

Books

AMENGUAL, BARTHÉLEMY. *George Wilhelm Pabst*. Cinéma d'Aujourd'hui #37, Paris: Editions Seghers, 1966. A brief monograph by the author, excerpts from critical writings, screenplays, and statements by Pabst, iconographical documents, and an exhaustive European bibliography.

BAINBRIDGE, JOHN. *Greta Garbo*. New York: Doubleday, 1955. This definitive biography of Garbo includes much background information on the making of Pabst's *Joyless Street* and his attempts to secure Garbo for the film.

BORDE, RAYMOND; BUACHE, FREDDY; and COURTADE, FRANCIS. *Le cinéma réaliste allemand*. Lyons: Serdoc, 1965. A reference volume with documentation and sequence breakdown of major German "realist" films, including major silent and sound films of Pabst.

BUACHE, FREDDY. "G. W. Pabst," *Premier Plan* No. 39. Lyons: Serdoc, 1965. Excellent brief monograph on Pabst's entire career, with a bias toward the early work and good accounts of the later French films.

EISNER, LOTTE H. *The Haunted Screen, Expressionism and the German Cinema*. Berkeley: University of California Press, 1969. Translation by Roger Greaves of *L'Ecran Démoniaque*. Superbly evocative critical-historical account of German film, with detailed appreciations of major Pabst films, especially *Pandora's Box* and *Threepenny Opera*. Includes an important account of Brecht and Weill's lawsuit.

HARTLAUB, GUSTAV F. "Zür Einfuhrung," *Die neue Sachlichkeit: Wanderausstellung der Stadtischen Kunsthalle zu Mannheim*. Dresden: Sachsischer Kunstverein, 1925. Important document related to an exhibition of German painters from October 18 to November 22, 1925, relating new social trends in art to *Die neue Sachlichkeit* (The New Objectivity).

HULL, DAVID STEWART. *Film in the Third Reich*. Berkeley: University of California Press, 1969. Incisive and well-written account of German Nazi cinema with informative and admiring accounts of Pabst's work, but with no indication of his actual dilemma.

155

JOSEPH, RUDOLPH S., ed., *Der Regisseur: G. W. Pabst.* München: 1963. Collection of brief essays, evaluations, and testimonies prepared for a retrospective exposition of Pabst's films at the Münchner Stadtmuseum, December 1963 to February 1964.

KRACAUER, SIEGFRIED. *From Caligari to Hitler: A Psychological History of the German Film.* Princeton, New Jersey: Princeton University Press, 1947. The author's detailed but tendentious account of Pabst's work is accurate, but tends toward an ideological bias, condemning him for "compromise."

ROTHA, PAUL. *The Film Till Now.* Third Edition. New York: Twayne Publishers, 1967. Although outmoded in some respects, the author displays unbounded enthusiasm and perceptivity for Pabst's early work, dismissing the later films with profound disillusionment.

WEIDELI, WALTER. *The Art of Bertolt Brecht.* Translated by Daniel Russell. New York: New York University Press, 1963. Excellent critical study of Brecht's work and its theatrical-philosophical significance, though only superficially concerned with his contribution to cinema.

———. *Classic Film Scripts: Pandora's Box (Lulu).* Translated by Christopher Holme. New York: Simon & Schuster, 1971. A translation, edited, with reference to an incomplete British archive (NFA) print, of Pabst's shooting script, with introductory essays by Louise Brooks ("Pabst and Lulu") and a chapter from Lotte Eisner's *The Haunted Screen.*

Parts of Books

AGEL, HENRI. *Les grands cinéastes.* Paris: Editions Universitaires, 1959. Collection of brief essays on historically important directors in world cinema, reflecting a typical European ambivalence toward Pabst in recent decades.

AUBRY, YVES and JACQUES PÉTAT. "G. W. Pabst," in *Anthologie du Cinéma,* Vol. 4. Paris: Editions l'Avant-Scène, 1968. Sketchy, but often penetrating monograph that assesses Pabst's major films. More lucid and better written than Amengual or Buache, though politically biased in regard to later works.

MANVELL, ROGER. *Film.* London: Penguin Press, 1946. A compendium of critical essays on film classics, including a richly evocative appraisal of *Kameradschaft.*

———. ed. "The Threepenny Opera," in *Masterpieces of the German Cinema.* Icon Editions. New York: Harper & Row, 1973. A historical introduction by Manvell to five complete scripts (including *M, The Golem, Nosferatu,* and *The Blue Angel*), including Paul Rotha's excellent appreciation of *Dreigroschenoper,* initially printed in 1933 in *Celluloid* (London).

MITRY, JEAN. *Histoire du cinéma: Art et industrie. III. 1923–1930.* Paris: Editions Universitaires. 1973. Although primarily concerned with their "realist" dimension, Mitry provides excellent accounts (pp. 223–33) of Pabst's major films while underscoring heavily their shortsighted ideological perspective.

PABST, G. W. "Servitude et grandeur de Hollywood," *Le rôle intellectual du cinéma.* Cahier 3. Paris: Institut international de cooperation culturelle, 1937. A scathing account by Pabst of the Hollywood system of film making during the 1930s which he found totally repressive and unproductive.

TYLER, PARKER. *Classics of the Foreign Film: A Pictorial Treasury.* New York: Citadel, 1962. Although primarily an illustrated text, the author's perceptive and eloquent essays on *Don Quichotte* and *The Threepenny Opera* are among the best on these films.

Magazine and Newspaper Articles

ANON. "*Skandal um Eva.*" *Close Up* 7, iii (September 1930), 221–22. A review of Pabst's Henny Porten vehicle, indicating his failure to transcend the formula-bound sentiments of the scenario.

ARISTARCO, GUIDO. "Il cinema tedesco e il passato nazista" (The German Cinema and its Nazi Past). *Cinestudio* 7, March, 1963. French translation in *Contre Champ* 6–7, 1963. An extremely critical account of Nazi and postwar German films, attacking Pabst and his films pitilessly for their artistic and ideological compromise.

ARNOUX, ALEXANDRE. "Un déjeuner avec Pabst." *Pour Vous* 115, January 29, 1931. An interview-discussion between Pabst and his scenarist for *L'Atlantide* and *Don Quichotte,* dealing with the director's political and social ideas as expressed in his work to date.

BACHMANN, GIDEON, ed. "Six Talks on G. W. Pabst." *Cinemages* 3, New York, 1955. A mimeographed transcription with annotated filmography of casual, informative, if often contradictory interviews with Pabst's former associates: Paul Falkenberg, Leo Lania, Ernö Metzner, Jean Oser, Eugen Schüfftan, and Marc Sorkin.

BROOKS, LOUISE. "Mr. Pabst." *Image* 5, vii (September 1956), 152–55. Informative and witty account of Brooks' encounter and working relationship with Pabst.

———. "Pabst and Lulu." *Sight & Sound* (Summer 1965), 123–27. The most important and perceptive essay on the conception and realization of Pabst's *Pandora's Box,* his working methods, and special artistic rapport with Louise Brooks.

BRYHER. "G. W. Pabst. A Survey." *Close Up* (December 1927), 56–61. An intelligent account of Pabst's silent work and its sociological and artistic relevance to cinema and the other arts. (Also an extensive article with photos on the production of *The Love of Jeanne Ney,* 17–26).

CARD, JAMES. "Out of Pandora's Box." *Image* 5, vii (September 1956), 148–152. An important reassessment of Pabst's films by the curator of film at George Eastman House, Rochester, New York, stressing his understanding of female psychology as opposed to social themes.

———. "The Intense Isolation of Louise Brooks." *Sight & Sound* 27 (Summer 1958), 241–244. A revelatory and fascinating account of the mysterious disappearance of Louise Brooks after her work with Pabst, her forced retirement, and "resurrection" under Card's careful guidance as a brilliant writer on Hollywood and the cinema.

CROCE, ARLENE. "The Threepenny Opera." *Film Quarterly* 14, i (Fall 1960), 43–45. A generally negative, though ambivalent appraisal of the reconstructed print, critical of musical omissions and the softening of the hard edges of the Brecht-Weill source.

DEL FRA, LINO, and GUERRINI TITO: "Vita e morte dell'hidalgo." *Filmcritica* 34–35 (March–April 1954), 138–44. An interesting Italian appraisal of *Don Quichotte*, drawing a parallel between the defeat of Cervantes' hero and that of Pabst, surrendering to commercial mediocrity.

GENESTE, RENÉ. "Dans son nouveau film 'Le Procès,' G. W. Pabst défend les Juifs . . . mais dix ans trop tard." *L'Ecran Français* 147 (April 20, 1948). A biased, negative review of Pabst's postwar film about Jewish pogroms in Hungary. ("In his new film, *The Trial*, G. W. Pabst defends the Jews . . . but Ten Years too Late.")

GERBE. LOUIS. "Les idées de Pabst sur le cinéma." *Je suis partout* 462 (January 19, 1933). The ideological weaknesses in Pabst's work are suggested by this French critic, though he finds Pabst's position in this interview nevertheless admirable.

KRASZNA–KRAUSZ, A. "G. W. Pabst's *Lulu*." *Close Up* 4, iv (April 1929), 24–30. Pabst's *Pandora's Box* is criticized on aesthetic grounds; the author finds Wedekind's verbal manner untranslatable into silent screen methods.

LANIA, LEO. "In Defense of Pabst." Letter to *The New York Times* (April 2, 1950), p. X, 4. A rather flat, weakly worked defense of Pabst's predicament of being forced to work for the Nazi regime though opposed to their goals.

LUFT, HERBERT. "G. W. Pabst." *Films in Review* 15 (February 1964), 93–109. A detailed historical account of Pabst's career and films, basically factual rather than critical.

———. "G. W. Pabst." *Films and Filming* 13, vii (April 1967), 18–24. Expanded version of previous article, with new interview material by the author.

POTAMKIN, HARRY ALAN. "Pabst and the Social Film." *Hound & Horn* 6 (January–March 1933), 284–298. A severely intellectual appraisal of the sociological dimension of Pabst's work, focusing on *The Threepenny Opera*. Strongly critical of Pabst's weaknesses.

STANBROOK, ALAN. "Great Films of the Century No. 10. *Die Dreigro-schenoper.*" *Films and Filming* 7, vii (April 1961), 15–17, 38. A detailed analysis of various aspects of Pabst's film: direction, script, setting, acting, critical evaluations. Questions whether it is an enduring work of art, or simply a "museum curio" of academic interest.

———. "Brecht et le cinéma." *Cahiers du cinéma* 114 (December 1960). A panoramic critical symposium with articles on Brecht's various encounters with cinema, including Pabst's "betrayal" of Brecht. Includes his original screen treatment for Pabst of "The Boss."

Unpublished Materials

LENNIG, ARTHUR. "The Joyless Street." A brief, pithy, and thoughtful analysis of the film, delineating the strengths of Pabst's work, especially compared with Griffith's *Isn't Life Wonderful?*

PABST, GERTRUDE. Letter to the author, dated September 13, 1976. An intimate account by Pabst's widow of the unfortunate circumstances of 1938–39 that led to their return to Austria where Pabst, who had planned to come to America, was obliged to remain and work during the war. No account is given (alas!) of the war years.

Filmography

Includes only films directed by Pabst. For a list of those in which he acted and those he scripted or supervised, see the Chronology at the front of the book. Unless otherwise noted, films for sale or rent in the United States are subtitled in English. No dubbed versions of any Pabst film are currently in circulation.

DER SCHATZ (The Treasure) (Froelich-Deulig, 1923)
Story: Rudolph Hans Bartsch
Scenario: G. W. Pabst and Willy Hennings
Camera: Otto Tober
Set Design: Walter Röhrig and Robert Herlth
Cast:
    Albert Steinrück (Balthasar, the Bellfounder)
    Ilka Grüning (Anna, his wife)
    Lucie Mannheim (Beatriz, their daughter)
    Hans Brausewetter (Arno, the goldsmith)
    Werner Krauss (John Svetelenz, the assistant)
Running time: 5 reels, ca. 75 mins.
Availability: *Not for sale or rent in U.S.A.*

GRÄFIN DONELLI (Countess Donelli) (Maxim Films, 1924)
Story and Scenario: Hans Kyser
Camera: Guido Seeber
Set Design: Hermann Warm
Cast:
    Henny Porten (Countess Donelli)
    Paul Hansen (Count Donelli)
    Friedrich Kayssler (Count Bergheim)
    Ferdinand von Alten (Baron von Trachwitz)
    Eberhard Leithoff (Ernst Hellwig, the young secretary)
    Lantelme Dürrer
Running time: 6 reels, ca. 81 mins.
Availability: Unavailable, reputedly lost.

DIE FREUDLOSE GASSE (The Joyless Street) (Sofar-Film-Produktion
   G.M.B.It. 1925)
Producers: M. Salkind and R. Pinès
Assistant Director: Marc Sorkin
Scenario: Willi Haas, from the novel by Hugo Bettauer
Camera: Guido Seeber, Kurt Oertel, Robert Lach
Set Design: Hans Sohnle, Otto Erdmann
Cast:
>   Greta Garbo (Greta Rumfort)
>   Asta Nielsen (Maria Lechner)
>   Einar Hanson (Lieutenant Davis, U.S.A.)
>   Werner Krauss (The Butcher of Melchoir Street)
>   Jaro Fürth (Councilor Rumfort)
>   Loni Nest (Rosa Rumfort)
>   Max Kohlhase (Maria's father)
>   Sylvia Torf (Maria's mother)
>   Karl Etlinger (Mr. Rosenow [or Lorring])
>   Ilka Grüning (his wife)
>   Countess Agnes Esterhazy (Regina, his daughter)
>   Alexander Mursky (Dr. Leid, a lawyer)
>   Tamara Tolstoi (Lia Leid)
>   Robert Garrison (Don Alfonso Cañez)
>   Henry Stuart (Egon Stirner, secretary to Mr. Rosenow)
>   Mario Cusmich (Colonel Irving, U.S.A.)
>   Valeska Gert (Frau Greifer)
>   Countess Tolstoi (Fraulein Henriette)
>   Edna Merkstein (Frau Merkel)
>   Hertha von Walther (Else)
>   Grigori Chmara (The Waiter)
>   Raskatoff (Trebitsch)
>   Krafft-Raschig (An American Soldier)
>   Otto Reinwald

A Post-Synchronized version was released in 1937 under the American
   title, *The Street of Sorrow.*
Running time: 8 reels, ca. 110 mins.
Availability: 16mm rental: Museum of Modern Art, New York (90-minute
   version); 8mm prints for sale by Niles Films of South Bend, Indiana,
   and other distributors.

GEHEIMNISSE EINER SEELE (Secrets of a Soul) (UFA, 1925)
Producer: Hans Neumann
Assistant Director: Mark Sorkin
Advisor: Dr. Nicholas Kaufmann

Scenario: Colin Ross and Hans Neumann, in collaboration with Dr. Hans
   Sachs and Karl Abraham
Camera: Guido Seeber, Kurt Oertel, Robert Lach
Set Design: Ernö Metzner
Cast:
   Werner Krauss (Martin Fellman)
   Ruth Weyher (his wife)
   Pawel Pawlow (Dr. Charles Orth, the psychoanalyst)
   Jack Trevor (Erich, the cousin)
   Ilka Grüning (The Mother)
   Hertha von Walther
   Renata Brausewetter
Running time: 6 reels, ca. 95 mins.
Availability: 16mm rental: MacMillan Films, Mount Vernon, New York

MAN SPIELT NICHT MIT DER LIEBE (One Does Not Play With Love)
   (F.P.S.-Phöbosfilm, 1926)
Assistant Director: Marc Sorkin
Story and Scenario: Willi Haas
Camera: Guido Seeber, Kurt Oertel, Robert Lach
Set Designs: Oscar Friedrich Werndorff
Musical Composition: Schmidt-Gentner
Cast:
   Lily Damita (Calixta Nepallek)
   Werner Krauss (Colalto)
   Erna Morena (Forence, ex-opera singer)
   Maria Paudler (Amina, a ballerina)
   Egon von Jordan (Eugen Lewis)
   Oreste Silancia (a friend)
   Arthur Retzback-Erasimy (Nepallek)
   Mathilde Sussin (Mrs. Lewis)
   Karl Ettlinger (Mr. Lewis)
Running time: 7 reels, ca. 91 mins.
Availability: Unavailable, reputedly lost.

DIE LIEBE DER JEANNE NEY (The Love of Jeanne Ney) (UFA, 1927)
Assistant Director: Marc Sorkin
Scenario: Ladislaus Vajda and Rudolf Leonhardt from the novel by Ilya
   Ehrenburg
Camera: Fritz Arno Wagner and Robert Lach
Set Design: Otto Hunte and Viktor Trivas
Cast:
   Edith Jehanne (Jeanne Ney)

Uno Henning (Andreas Labov)
Fritz Rasp (Khalibiev)
Brigitte Helm (Gabrielle)
Adolph Edgar Licho (Raymond Ney)
Eugen Jensen (André Ney, the father)
Hans Jaray (Poitras)
Siegfried Arno (Ney's detective)
Hertha von Walther (Margo)
Vladimir Sokoloff (Zacharkiewicz)
Running time: 9 reels, ca. 114 mins.
Availability: 16mm rental: Museum of Modern Art, New York; Macmillan
Films.

ABWEGE (Crisis) or **BEGIERDE** (Desire) (Erda Films, 1928)
Assistant Director: Marc Sorkin
Story and Scenario: Franz Schulz, Adolf Lantz, Ladislaus Vajda
Camera: Theodor Sparkuhl
Set Design: Hans Sohnle and Otto Erdmann
Cast:
    Brigitte Helm (Irene)
    Gustav Diessl (Robert Storner [or Thomas Beck])
    Hertha von Walther (Liane, Irene's friend)
    Jack Trevor (Walter Frank, the painter)
    Nico Turoff (Sam Taylor, the boxer)
    Fritz Odemar (Manners)
Running time: 8 reels, ca. 107 mins.
Availability: *Not available for rent or sale in U.S.A.*

DIE BÜCHSE DER PANDORA (Pandora's Box) (Nero Films, 1928)
Producers: Seymour Nebenzahl, George C. Horsetzky.
Assistant Directors: Marc Sorkin, Paul Falkenberg.
Scenario: Ladislaus Vajda from the plays *Erdgeist* and *Die Büchse der Pan-
    dora* by Frank Wedekind.
Camera: Günther Krampf.
Set Design: Andrei Andreiev
Costumes: Gottlieb Hesch
Cast:
    Louise Brooks (Lulu)
    Gustav Diessl (Jack the Ripper)
    Fritz Kortner (Dr. Peter Schön)
    Franz Lederer (Alva Schön)
    Carl Goetz (Schigolch)
    Krafft-Raschig (Rodrigo Quast)
    Alice Roberts (Countess Anna Geschwitz)

Daisy d'Ora (Marie de Zarniko)
Michael von Newlinsky (Marquis of Casti-Piani)
Siegfried Arno (The Stage Director)
Running time: original version, 131 mins., cut to 8 reels, 120 mins.
Availability: 16mm rental: Janus Films, New York.

DIE WEISSE HÖLLE VOM PITZ-PALU (The White Hell of Pitz-Palu)
(Aaga Films/Sokal, 1929)
Co-Director and Scenarist: Dr. Arnold Fanck
Assistant Director: Marc Sorkin
Scenario: Ladislaus Vajda
Camera: Sepp Allgeier, Hans Schneeberger, Richard Angst
Set Design: Ernö Metzner
Cast:
    Leni Riefenstahl (Maria, the fiancée)
    Ernst Peterson (Karl Stern)
    Gustav Diessl (Dr. Johannes Krafft)
    Mizzi Gotzel (Maria Krafft)
    Otto Spring (Christian Klucker, guide)
    Ernst Udel (The Aviator)
    Kurt Gerron (man in the bar)
The film was reissued in 1935 with a synchronized music score by Giuseppi
    Becce.
Running time: 8 reels, ca. 90 mins.
Availability: 16mm rental: Museum of Modern Art, New York; Universal-
    16, New York. 8mm prints sold by Cinema 8, Chester, Connecticut,
    and Milestone Movie Company, Monroe, Connecticut.

DAS TAGEBUCH EINER VERLORENEN (Diary of a Lost Girl) (Pabst-
    Film G.M.B.H., 1929).
Assistant Directors: Marc Sorkin and Paul Falkenberg
Scenario: Rudolf Leonhardt, from the novel by Margarethe Boehme
Camera: Sepp Allgeier
Set Design: Ernö Metzner and Emil Hasler
Cast:
    Louise Brooks (Thymiane Henning)
    Edith Meinhard (Erika)
    Vera Pawlowa (Aunt Frieda)
    Joseph Rovensky (Henning, the pharmacist)
    Fritz Rasp (Meinert, his assistant)
    André Roanne (Count Osdorff)
    Arnold Korff (The Elderly Count Osdorff)
    Andrews Engelmann (Director of the Reform School)
    Valeska Gert (his wife)

Franciska Kinz (Meta)
Sybille Schmitz (Elizabeth, the first governess)
Siegfried Arno (a guest)
Kurt Gerron (Dr. Vitalis)
Running time: 130 mins.
Availability: *Not available for sale or rent in U.S.A.*

WESTFRONT 1918 (Nero Films, 1930)
Assistant Producer: H. Landsmann
Assistant Director: Marc Sorkin
Scenario: Ladislaus Vajda and Peter Martin Lampel from the novel, *Vier von der Infanterie* by Ernst Johannsen
Camera: Fritz Arno Wagner and Charles Métain
Set Designs: Ernö Metzner
Sound: Guido Bagier (Tobis Kangfilm System)
Cast:
    Gustav Diessl (Karl)
    Fritz Kampers (The Bavarian)
    Hans Joachim Moebis (The Student)
    Claus Clausen (The Lieutenant)
    Gustav Püttjer (The Hamburg Man)
    Jackie Monnier (Yvette)
    Hanna Hoessrich (Karl's wife)
    Else Heller (Karl's mother)
    Carl Balhaus (The Butcher Boy)
    Vladimir Sokoloff (An orderly)
    Also: Aribert Mog, André Saint-Germain
Running time: 90 mins.
Availability: 16mm rental: Museum of Modern Art, New York.

SKANDAL UM EVA (Scandalous Eva) (Nero-Porten Films, 1930)
Assistant Director: Marc Sorkin
Scenario: Friedrich Raff and Julius Urgiss from *Skandal um Olly* by Heinrich Ilgenstein
Camera: Fritz Arno Wagner
Set Design: Franz Schrödter
Sound: Guido Bagier (Tobis Klangfilm System)
Cast:
    Henny Porten (Dr. Eva Rutgers)
    Oskar Sima (Dr. Kurt Hiller, minister of education)
    Ludwig Stössel (Dr. Rohrback)
    Paul Henckels (Professor Hagen)
    Adele Sandrola (Vulpius)
    Fritz Odemar (Lämmerberg)

Käthe Haack (Käte Brandt)
Claus Clausen (Schlotterbeck)
Frigga Grant (Mrs. Schlotterbeck)
Karl Etlinger (Steinlechner)
Availability: Unavailable, reputedly lost.

DIE DREIGROSCHENOPER (The Threepenny Opera) (Warner
   Brothers/Nero-Films/Tobis, 1931)
Producer: Seymour Nebenzahl
Assistant Director: Marc Sorkin
Scenario: Ladislaus Vajda, Leo Lania and Bela Balàsz from the Berthold
   Brecht-Kurt Weill play, inspired by John Gay's *The Beggar's Opera*
Adaptors (French version): Solange Bussi, André Mauprey, Ninon Steinhoff
Camera: Fritz Arno Wagner
Set Design: Andrei Andreiev
Film Editors: Hans Oser (German version); Henri Rust (French version)
Sound: Adolph Jansen (Tobis Klangfilm)
Orchestrations: Theo Mackeben
Cast: *German version* (113 mins.)
   Rudolf Forster (Mackie Messer)
   Carola Neher (Polly Peachum)
   Valeska Gert (Mrs. Peachum)
   Reinold Schünzel (Tiger-Brown)
   Fritz Rasp (Peachum)
   Lotte Lenya (Jenny)
   Hermann Thimig (The Pastor)
   Ernst Busch (Strassensänger)
   Vladimir Sokoloff (Smith, the jailer)
   Paul Kemp
   Gustav Püttjer
   Oskar Höcker
   Krafft-Raschig (Mackie's gang)
   Herbert Grünbaum (Filch)
Cast: *French version* (104 mins.)
   Albert Préjean (Mackie Messer)
   Odette Florelle (Polly Peachum)
   Gaston Modot (Peachum)
   Jane Marken (Mrs. Peachum)
   Jacques Henley (Tiger-Brown)
   Margo Lion (Jenny)
   Bill Bockett (Strassensänger)
   Vladimir Sokoloff (Smith, the jailer)
   Antonin Artaud (the apprentice beggar)
   Hermann Thimig (The Pastor)

Arthur Duarte, Marcel Merminod, Pierre Léaud, Albert Broquin
    (Mackie's gang)
Marie-Antoine Buzet, and Préjeanne.
Availability: 16mm rental: MacMillan Films, Mount Vernon, New York.

KAMERADSCHAFT (Comradeship) (Nero Films AG/ Gaumont/ Franco-
    Film-Aubert, 1931)
Producer: Seymour Nebenzahl
Assistant Director: Herbert Rappoport
Advisor for French sequences: Robert Beaudoin
Scenario: Ladislaus Vajda, Karl Otten, and Peter Martin Lampel from a
    story outline by Karl Otten.
Camera: Fritz Arno Wagner and Robert Baberske
Set Design: Erno Metzner and Karl Vollbrecht
Film Editor: Hans Oser
Cast:
    Ernst Busch (Wittkopp, a German miner)
    Elisabeth Wendt (his wife)
    Alexander Granach (Kaspers)
    Fritz Kampers (Wilderer)
    Gustav Püttjer (Kaplan)
    Georges Charlia (Jean, a French miner)
    Andrée Ducret (Françoise)
    Daniel Mandaille (Emile, her brother)
    Alex Bernard (The Grandfather)
    Pierre Louis (Georges)
    Héléna Manson (wife of a wounded miner)
    Also: Oskar Höcker, Marcel Lesueur, André Nicolle, Georges Tour-
        reil, Marguerite Dubos
Running time: 93 mins.
Availability: 16mm rental: MacMillan Films, Mount Vernon, New York.

L'ATLANTIDE (Die Herrin von Atlantis) (Nero Films, 1932)
Producer: Seymour Nebenzahl
Assistant Director: Marc Sorkin
Scenario: Alexandre Arnoux, Jacques Duval, Ladislaus Vajda, from the
    novel by Pierre Benoit.
Adaptation (German version): Ladislaus Vajda and Hermann Oberkander
Camera: Eugen Schüfftan, Ernst Koerner
Dialogue: Jacques Duval
Set Design: Ernö Metzner
Costumes: M. Pretzfelder and Pierre Ichac
Film Editor: Hans Oser
Music Score: Wolfgang Zeller

Sound: Adolf Jansen
Cast: *German version*
    Brigitte Helm (Antinéa)
    Gustav Diessl (Morhange)
    Tela Tschai (Tanit-Zerga)
    Heinz Klingenberg (Saint-Avit)
    Mathias Wiemann (The Norwegian)
    Vladimir Sokoloff (Count Bielowsky, Hetman of Jitomir)
    Georges Tourreil (an officer)
    Odette Florelle (Clémentinéa)
Cast: *French version*
    Brigette Helm (Antinéa)
    Jean Angelo (Captain Morhange)
    Tela Tschai (Tanit-Zerga)
    Pierre Blanchar (Lieutenant Saint-Avit)
    Mathias Wiemann (The Norwegian)
    Vladimir Sokoloff (Count Bielowsky, Hetman of Jitomir)
    Georges Tourreil (Lieutenant Ferrières)
    Odette Florelle (Clémentinéa)
Running time: 90 minutes.
Availability: *Not available for rent or sale in U.S.A.*
An English-language version was also filmed, with Brigitte Helm and Gustav Diessl, playing the leads. Marc Sorkin edited this version for release by Universal.

DON QUICHOTTE (Don Quixote) (Vandor-Nelson-Webster, 1933)
Director of Production: Constantin Geftman
Assistant Director: Jean de Limur
Scenario and Dialogue: Paul Morand and Alexandre Arnoux, from the novel of Miguel de Cervantes
Camera: Nikolas Farkas and Paul Portier
Settings: Andrei Andreiev; Chinese Shadows: Lotte Reiniger
Costumes: M. Pretzfelder
Music Score: Jacques Ibert
Film Editor: Hans Oser
Cast: *French version*
    Fédor Chaliapin (Don Quixote)
    Dorville (Sancho Panza)
    Renée Valliers (Dulcinea)
    Mady Berry (Sancho's wife)
    Mireille Balin (The Duchess)
    Also: Arlette Marchal, Vladimir Sokoloff, René Donnio, Mafer, Jean Martinelli, Charles Léger, Pierre Labry, Jean de Limur, Leo Larive, Genica Athanasiou.

The English language version starred Chaliapin and George Robey as Sancho Panza.
Running time: 83 minutes.
Availability: *Not available for sale or rental in U.S.A.*

DU HAUT EN BAS (High and Low) (Tobis Films/Pabst, 1933)
Scenario: Anna Greuyner from the play by Ladislaus Bus-Fekete.
Dialogue: Georges Dolley
Camera: Eugen Schüfftan
Settings: Ernö Metzner
Music Score: Marcel Lattès
Film Editor: Jean (Hans) Oser
Song: Herbert Rappoport and André Michel (also assistant directors)
Cast:
 Michel Simon (M. Bodeletz, the old gambler)
 Margo Lion (Madame Binder)
 Mauricet (M. Binder, her fourth husband)
 Jean Gabin (Charles Boulla)
 Georges Morton (Charles' uncle, the concierge)
Running time: 79 mins.
Availability: *Not available for sale or rent in U.S.A.*

A MODERN HERO (Warner Brothers, U.S.A., 1934)
Screenplay: Gene Markey and Katherine Scola from the novel by Louis Bromfield
Camera: William Rees
Settings: Cedric Gibbons
Film Editor: Jim Gibbons
Cast:
 Richard Barthelmess (Pierre Radier)
 Jean Muir (Joanna Ryan)
 Dorothy Burgess (Hazel Rodier)
 Marjorie Rambeau (Madame Azais)
 Florence Eldridge (Leah)
 Theodore Newton (Elmer)
 William Janney (Young Pierre)
 Verree Teasdale (Claire Benson)
 Maidel Turner (Aunt Clara)
 J. M. Kerrigan (Ryan)
Running time: 70 mins.
Availability: 16mm rental: United Artists/16, New York

MADEMOISELLE DOCTEUR (or Salonique, nid d'espions) (Romain Pinès-Films/ Trocadéro, 1936).

Producer: Constantin Geftman
Assistant Director: André Michel
Scenario: Yan Cube, Leo Birinsky, Hermann Mankiewicz
Adaptation: Georges Neveu and Jacques Natanson
Dialogue: Jacques Natanson
Camera: Eugen Schüfftan and Paul Portier
Settings: Serge Pimenoff and René Hubert
Film Editor: Marc Sorkin
Music Score: Arthur Honegger and C. Oberfeld
Orchestral Direction: Maurice Jaubert
Sound: Teisseire
Cast:
> Dita Parlo (Mademoiselle Docteur)
> Pierre Blanchar (Condojan)
> Pierre Fresnay (Captain Carrère)
> Louis Jouvet (Simonis)
> Charles Dullin (Matthesius)
> Viviane Romance (Gaby)
> Roger Karl (Colonel Bourget)
> Ernest Ferny (Major Jacquart)
> Jean-Louis Barrault (The Melon Man)
> Gaston Modot (cafe proprietor)
> Jacques Henley (U.S. Consul)

An English-language version was made in 1937 by Edmond-T. Gréville, with Erich von Stroheim as Condojan.
Running time: 95 mins.
Availability: *Not available for rent or sale in U.S.A.*

LE DRAME DE SHANGHAI (Shanghai Drama) (Lucia Films/ Gladiator, 1938)
Producer: R. Pinès
Scenario and Adaptation: Leo Lania and Henri Jeanson from O.-P. Gilbert's *Shanghai, chambard et Cie*
Dialogue: Henri Jeanson
Camera: Eugen Schüfftan and Louis Page
Settings: Andrei Andreiev
Costumes: Georges Annenkoff and Gastyne
Film Editor: Jean (Hans) Oser
Music Score: Ralph Erwin
Sound: Teisseire
Cast:
> Louis Jouvet (Ivan)
> Christiane Mardayne (Kay, the spy)
> Elina Labourdette (Vera, her daughter)

Raymond Rouleau (Franchon)
Dorville (Bill, a former convict)
Suzanne Desprès (Nana)
Gabrielle Dorziat (The Superintendent)
Mila Parely (The Dancer)
My Linh-Nam (Tcheng)
Vladimir Inkijinoff (agent of the "Black Dragons")
Running time: 100 mins.
Availability: *Not available for rent or sale in U.S.A.*

JEUNES FILLES EN DETRESS (Girls in Distress) (Globe Films, 1939)
Producer: Arnold Mivrach
Assistant Directors: André Michel, Jacqueline Audry
Scenario and Adaptation: Christa Winslow, from a novel by Peter Quinn
Dialogue: Jean-Bernard Luc
Camera: Michel Kelber and Marcel Weiss
Settings: Andrei Andreiev
Costumes: Jacques Manuel
Musical Score: Ralph Erwin
Cast:
    André Luguet (Monsieur Presle)
    Marcelle Chantal (Madame Presle)
    Micheline Presle (Jacqueline, their daughter)
    Jacqueline Delubac (Madame Paule d'Ivry)
    Louise Carletti (Margot, her daughter)
    Aquistapace (The Minister)
    Robert Pisani (Monsieur Tarrand)
Availability: *Not available for rent or sale in U.S.A.*

KOMÖDIANTEN (Comedians) (Bavaria Films/München, 1941)
Scenario: Axel Eggebrecht, Walter von Hollander and Pabst, from the
    novel *Philine,* by Olly Boeheim
Camera: Bruno Stephan
Settings: Julius von Borsody and Hans Hochreiter
Costumes: Maria Pommer-Pehl
Film Editor: Rudolph Griesebach
Musical Score: Lothar Bruhne
Sound: Emil Specht
Technical Directors: Willy Laschinsky and Theo Kaspar
Cast:
    Käthe Dorsch (Karoline Neuber)
    Hilde Krahl (Philine Schröder)
    Henny Porten (Amalia, Duchess of Wissenfels)
    Gustav Diessl (Ernst Biron)

Ludwig Schmitz (Müller Hanswurst, the harlequin)
Richard Haussler (Armin von Perckhammer)
Friedrich Domin (Johann Neuber)
Sonja-Gerda Scholz (The Feigin)
Lucie Millowitsch (The Loren)
Bettina Hambach (Victorine)
Running time: 120 mins.
Availability: For sale or rent, in versions with or without English subtitles, by Twyman Films, Dayton, Ohio.

PARACELSUS (Bavaria Films/München, 1943)
Producer: Fred Lyssa
Assistant Director: Auguste Barth-Reuss
Scenario: Kurt Heuser and Pabst from the novel *König der Arzte*, by Pert Peternell
Camera: Bruno Stephan
Settings: Herbert Hochreiter and Walter Schlick
Film Editor: Lena Neumann
Music Score: Herbert Windt
Sound: Emil Specht
Costumes: Herbert Ploberger
Cast:
Werner Krauss (Paracelsus)
Mathias Wiemann (Ulrich von Hutten)
Harald Kreutzberg (Fliegenbein, the harlequin)
Martin Urtel (Johannes Famulus)
Harry Langewisch (Pfefferkorn, the rich merchant)
Annelies Reinhold (Renata, his wife)
Fritz Rasp (The Schoolmaster)
Josef Sieber (Bilse, Paracelsus' valet)
Herbert Hübner (Count von Hohenried)
Rudolf Blümner (Forben, the printer)
Karl Skraup (The Surgeon)
Franz Schafheitlin (Erasmus)
Availability: Running time: 106 mins.
For sale or rent, either with or without English subtitles, by Twyman Films, Dayton, Ohio.

DER FALL MOLANDER (The Case of Molander) (Terra Films/Prague, 1944)
(Left incomplete with the Russian invasion of Prague and now believed destroyed in a bombing of a laboratory where post-production work was in progress.)

Scenario: Ernst Hasselbach and Per Schwenzen from the novel *Die Sterne-
    geige* by Alfred Karrasch
Camera: Willy Kuhle
Music: Werner Eisbrenner
Cast:
    Paul Wegener, Irene von Meyendorff, Robert Tessen, Werner Hinz,
    Erich Ponto, Evan Maria Meinecke, Harald Paulsen, Elisabeth Mar-
    kus, Heinz Moog, Wilfried Seyferth, Viktor Afritsch, Ernst Fritz Für-
    bringer, Will Dohm, Rudolf Schündler, Walter Richter, Walter
    Franck, Walter Werner, Theodor Loos, Fritz Odemar, Karl Skraup,
    Harry Langewisch, Hermine Ziegler

DER PROZESS (The Trial) (Hübler-Kahla Filmpoduktion/ Vienna, 1947).
Producer: J. A. Beyer
Assistant Directors: Georges Reuther, Hermann Lanske, Walter Meiners
Scenario: Kurt Heuser, Rudolf Brunngraber, Emeric Roboz from the novel,
    Prozess auf Leben und Tod by Brunngraber
Camera: Oskar Schnirch and Helmut Fischer-Ashley
Settings: Werner Schlichting
Film Editor: Anna Höllering
Music Score: Alois Melichar
Cast:
    Ernst Deutsch (Peczely Scharf, the Rabbi)
    Ewald Balser (Dr. Eötvös)
    Aglaja Schmid (Esther Solymosi)
    Albert Truby (Moritz Scharf)
    Gustav Diessl (Both)
    Marianne Schönauer (Julia)
    Joseph Meinrad (Bary)
    Maria Eis (M. Solymosi)
    Ernst Waldbrunn (Wollner)
    Heinz Moog (Baron Onody)
    Ivan Petrevich (Egressy)
    Eva-Maria Skala (Julca)
    Ladislaus Morgenstern (Salomon Schwartz)
    Ida Russka (Batori)
    Leopold Rudolf (Reszky)
    Also: Max Brod, Hintz Fabricus, Pepi Glöckner-Kramer, Harry
        Rameau-Pulvermacher
Running time: 109 mins.
Availability: *Not available for sale or rent in U.S.A.*

GEHEIMNISVOLLE TIEFEN (Mysterious Shadows) (Pabst-Kiba Film-
    produktion/Vienna, 1949)
Scenario: Trude Pabst and Walter von Hollander

Camera: Hans Schneeberger and Helmut Fischer-Ashley
Settings: Werner Schlichting and Isabella Ploberger
Musical Score: Roland Kova
Musical Director: Alois Melichar
Cast:
> Paul Hubschmid (Dr. Ben Wittich)
> Ilse Werner (Cornelia, his fiancee)
> Stefan Skodler (Robert Roy, the fat industrialist)
> Elfe Gerhart (Charlotte, his friend)
> Hermann Thimig (Heineman)
> Maria Eis (Madame Willard, Roy's associate)

Running time: 109 mins.
Availability: *Not available for sale or rent in U.S.A.*

LA VOCE DEL SILENZIO (The Voice of Silence) (Cines/ Franco/ London Film/ Rome, 1952)
Director of Production: Silvio d'Amico
Production Supervisor: Carlo Civallero
Assistant Directors: Bruno Paolinelli and Serge Vallin.
Story: Cesare Zavattini
Scenario: G. W. Pabst, Guiseppi Berto, Oreste Biancolo, Tullio Pinelli, Giorgio Prosperi, Pierre Bost, Roland Laudenbach, Akos Tolnay, Pietro Tompkins, Franz Treuberg, Bonaventura Tecchi, Jean Cocteau
Camera: Gabor Pogani
Settings: Guido Fiorini
Film Editor: Eraldo da Roma
Music: Enzo Mazetti; Directed by Fernando Previtale
Cast:
> Aldo Fabrizi (The Candle Maker)
> Jean Marais (The Partisan)
> Franck Villard (The Novelist)
> Daniel Gélin (The Repatriate)
> Paolo Stoppa (The Publisher)
> Eduardo Cianelli (The Abbe)
> Paolo Panelli (The Thief)
> Fernando Fernand Gomès (The Priest)
> Antonio Crast (The Religious Teacher)
> Checco Durante (The Sexton)
> Cosetta Greco (The Repatriate's Wife)
> Maria Grazia Francia (The Candle Maker's daughter)
> Rossana Podestà (The girl in the catacomb)
> Enrico Luzzi

Running time: 90 mins.
Availability: *Not available for rent or sale in U.S.A.*

COSE DA PAZZI (Crazy Affairs) (Kronos Films/Italy, 1953)
Producer: Bruno Paolinelli
Scenario: Bruno Paolinelli, B. Valeri, Leo Lania
Camera: Mario Bava and Gabor Pogani
Cast:
  Aldo Fabrizi (The Wise Madman)
  Carla del Poggio (The Student)
  Enrico Luzi (The Young Doctor on TV)
  Enrico Viarisio (The Director of the Clinic)
Availability: *Not available for rent or sale in U.S.A.*

DAS BEKENNTNIS DER INA KAHR (The Confession of Ina Kahr)
  (Omega Films/ West Germany, 1954).
Producer: August Barth-Reuss
Scenario: Erna Fentsch from the novel by Hans Emil Dits
Camera: Günthers Anders
Settings: Otto Pischinger and Herta Hareiter
Film Editor: Herbert Taschner
Musical Score: Erwin Halletz
Cast:
  Curt Jürgens (Paul Kahr)
  Elisabeth Müller (Ina, his wife)
  Albert Lieven (Dr. Pleyer, lawyer)
  Vera Molnar (Jenny)
  Jester Naefe (Cora Brink)
  Hanna Rucker (Helga Barnholm)
  Friedrich Domin (Father Stoll)
  Margit Trooger (Margit Kahr)
  Ingmar Zeisberg (Marianne von Degenhardt)
  Hilde Körber (Stuckmann, the guardian)
Running time: 102 mins.
Availability: *Not available for sale or rent in U.S.A.*

DER LETZTE AKT (U.S.A., *The Last Ten Days;* United Kingdom, *Ten Days to Die*) (Cosmopol Film, 1955)
Producer: Karl Szokoll
Scenario: Fritz Habeck, from a screenplay by Erich Maria Remarque, inspired by Michael A. Musmano's journal of the International Tribunal at Nuremburg, *Ten Days to Die.*
Camera: Günther Anders and Hannes Staudiger
Set design: Werner Schlichting, C   Pischinger, Wolf Witzemann
Film Editor: Harbert Taschner
Musical score: Erwin Haletz
Sound: Otto Untersalmberger
Makeup: Rudolf Ohlschmidt and Leopold Kuhnert

Cast:
  Albin Skoda (Adolf Hitler)
  Lotte Tobisch (Eva Braun)
  Willy Krauss (Josef Goebbels)
  Elga Dohrn (Magda Goebbels)
  Hermann Erhardt (Herman Goering)
  Eric Suckmann (Heinrich Himmler)
  Kurt Eilers (Martin Bormann)
  Julius Jonak (SS-Obergruppenfuhrer Hermann Fegelein)
  Leopold Hainisch (Marshal Keitel)
  Walter Regelsberger (Major Venner)
  Ernst Waldbrunn (Hitler's astrologer)
  Ernst Pröckl (Gauleiter Wagner)
  Gerd Zöhling (Richard, the young soldier)
  Oskar Werner (Captain Wurst)
  Eric Frey (General Burgdorf)
  Hannes Schiel (Guenoche, SS Officer)
  Herbert Herbe (General Krebs)
  Otto Schmöle (General Alfred Jodl)
  Otto Wögerer (General Ritter von Greim)
  Erland Erlandsen (Minister Albert Speer)
Running time: 109 mins.
Availability: 16mm rental: MacMillan Films, Mount Vernon, New York.

ES GESCHAH AM 20 JULI (It Happened on July 20; British title, *Jackboot Mutiny*) (Arca-Ariston Films, 1955)
Producers: Jochen Genzow and Frank Seitz
Scenario: Werner P. Zibaso and Gustav Machaty from the testimony of Jochen Wilke
Camera: Kurt Hasse
Settings: Ernst H. Albrecht and P. Markwitz
Commentary: Sam Wanamaker
Film Editor: Herbert Taschner
Music Score: Johannes Weissenbach
Sound: Felix Fohn, Walter Zander
Cast:
  Bernard Wicki (Count Stauffenberg)
  Karl Ludwig Diehl (General Beck)
  Carl Very (General Fromm)
  Kurt Meisel (Lieutenant General-SS)
  Erik Frey (General Olbricht)
  Albert Hehn (Major Remer)
  Til Kive (Lieutenant von Häften)
  Jochem Hauer (Field-Marshal Keitel)
  Oliver Hassencamp (Lieutenant Rohricht)

Running time: 87 mins.
Availability: *Not available for sale or rent in U.S.A.*

ROSEN FÜR BETTINA (Roses for Bettina) Carlton Films/AF Films, 1956)
Producer: Klauss Stapenhorst
Scenario: Werner P. Zibaso and G. D. Andam
Camera: Franz Koch
Settings: Otto Pischinger and Herta Hareither
Film Editor: Lilian Seng
Costumes: Theodor Rossi-Turai
Choreography: Alan Carter
Music: Herbert Windt, and selections from Tchaikowsky and Ravel
Sound: Carl Pecker
Cast:
    Elisabeth Müller (Bettina Sanden)
    Willy Birgel (Forster)
    Ivan Desny (Kostja Tomkoff, the choreographer)
    Eva Kerbler (Irene Gerwing)
    Carl Wery (Dr. Brinkmann)
    Hermann Speelmans (Kalborn)
    Erich Ponto (Schimansky)
    Leonard Steckel (Director of the Opera)

DURCH DIE WALDER, DURCH DIE AUEN (Through the Forests,
    Through the Fields) (Unicorn, 1956).
Producer: André Barth-Reuss
Scenario: G. W. Pabst and W. P. Zibaso
Camera: Kurt Brigoleit (color)
Cast: Eva Bartok, Karl Schönböck, Michael Cramer, Peter Ahrens, Rudoph
    Vogel, Joe Stöckl

    NOTE: Some 16mm prints of German feature films—some with En-
    glish subtitles, some without—are available free for classroom use
    from the Embassy of the Federal Republic of Germany,
    Washington, D.C.

Index

179